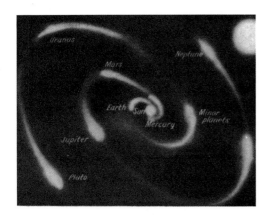

THE WONDER BOOK

OF

WOULD YOU
BELIEVE IT?

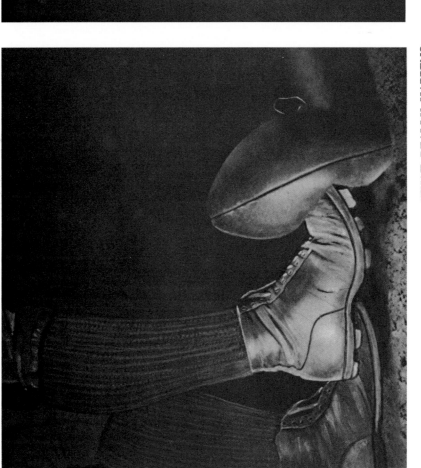

WHAT REALLY HAPPENS.

A Football at the Moment of Impact.   A Tennis-ball in Contact with a Racquet.

High-speed photographs taken by Harold E. Egerton and Kenneth J. Germeshangen at the Massachusetts Institute of Technology.
These pictures were given an exposure of only 1—100,000th of a second.   The football is fully inflated, and the white object on the racquet is a tennis-ball—not a poached egg !

THE WONDER BOOK

OF

WOULD YOU BELIEVE IT?

WITH EIGHT COLOUR PLATES
AND NEARLY THREE HUNDRED ILLUSTRATIONS

General Editor : HARRY GOLDING, F.R.G.S.

WARD, LOCK & CO., LIMITED
LONDON AND MELBOURNE

The information provided in this book is a general overview of the games, sports, activities and facets as recommended and published in 1936. The Publishers shall have no liability with respect to any harm, loss or damage, caused by, or alleged to be caused by, or in any way arising from, or alleged to be arising from information contained in this book. It is not an instruction manual and is presented as general information and should not be considered as a replacement for qualified and professional advice.

First published in Great Britain by Ward Lock & Co., Limited
This edition first published in Great Britain in 2008 by Cassell Illustrated,
a division of Octopus Publishing Group Ltd,
2–4 Heron Quays, London E14 4JP

Text, layout and design copyright © 2008 Octopus Publishing Group Limited
Octopus Publishing Group is a division of Hatchette Livre (UK)

Distributed in the U.S. and Canada by Octopus Books USA:
c/o Hachette Book Group USA
237 Park Avenue
New York NY 10017

A CIP catalogue record for this book is available from the British Library.

ISBN-13: 978-1-844-03655-4

Production: Caroline Alberti
Publisher: Mathew Clayton

Printed and bound in China

10 9 8 7 6 5 4 3 2 1

AN OCTOPUS ATTACKING A LOBSTER

COLOUR PLATES

[E.N.A.

Natives of Kashmir with their strange boats, made of inflated bullock skins, on the river Sutlej.

CONTENTS

CONTENTS

Mondiale]   *[Robert McLeod.*

WHAT ARE THEY?
Baby Hedgehogs.

A GIANT.

One of three giant heads cut out of the granite face of Mount Rushmore, South Dakota, U.S.A. This one, which measures 66 feet from chin to crown, represents Abraham Lincoln. The other heads, which together with this form a " Shrine of Democracy," are those of George Washington and Thomas Jefferson. A fourth head—that of Theodore Roosevelt, is to be added.

9

[*A. Brooker Klugh.*

THE STAR-NOSED MOLE (*Condylura cristata*).
A North American species. Its chief peculiarity lies in the tip of the snout, which is provided with a number of radiating tactile filaments.

10

AN AFRICAN MIRACLE

The Bismarck Rocks in Lake Victoria Nyanza, Tanganyika, an hour before the arrival of a "Floating Island," the name given locally to a natural phenomenon which renders Lake Victoria a miraculous and sacred sheet of water to the native mind.

Photos] [*E.N.A.*

After the arrival of the "Floating Island," which is really an accumulation of vegetation suddenly and periodically blown up round the rocks by the wind. It grows rapidly and makes it appear as though an island had risen out of the water.

SQUIDS.   [*Raoul Barba.*

Some squids are luminescent, and one of them has the strange power of squirting out luminous fluid into the water surrounding it : the exact opposite of the octopus' habit of squirting " ink."

CREATURES THAT PRODUCE THEIR OWN "COLD" LIGHT

ODD though it may seem, the most efficient known producer of light is neither the sun, nor the stars, nor even a modern electric lamp, but the firefly or glow-worm. All ordinary sources of light are hot. That means that a great part of their energy is wasted as heat. The glow-worm's radiation, on the other hand, consists practically entirely of light, so that it may be said to produce " cold " light. Electrical engineers would be delighted if they could do only half as well.

This power of producing light with almost perfect efficiency is possessed equally by the true fireflies of tropical America, which are still used by the natives in some parts as lamps, and by the less vivid glow-worm of England. It is virtually certain that the light comes in each case from some slow process of chemical change. This also is the origin of the light emitted by slow-burning phosphorus, which can be seen glowing with a greenish-yellow colour in the dark.

It is from the glow of phosphorus that the term phosphorescence is derived, and anyone would naturally imagine that phosphorus itself was phosphorescent. So, of course, it ought to be if the name had been well chosen. But, in fact, scientists have chosen to apply the term phosphorescent to a somewhat different form of light production. This phosphorescence is the power possessed by some materials to glow after exposure to light ; or the term may be applied to radiation of other kinds. Phosphorus itself, and for that matter the firefly, has no need of such refreshment and so is not, strictly speaking, phosphorescent. Luminous paint, such as is used on watch-dials, is the most familiar example of true phosphorescence.

One form of luminous paint is made from calcium sulphide, closely mixed with about two parts in a hundred of salt and a trace of some metal, such as copper or manganese. This will glow after it has been

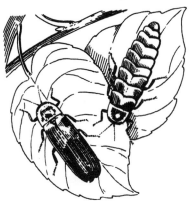

exposed to light, but not otherwise, so a minute quantity of radium is added to the paint as a perpetual stimulus. Whether in light or darkness, the radiation from the radium is continually bombarding the rest of the paint so that it will glow, even if kept permanently in the dark.

Most, and in fact probably all, living things which shine in the dark get their light, like the glow-worm, from some form of chemical change. There are very many examples, but the strangest of all are perhaps the many coloured lights carried by deep-sea fish. The American scientist,

GLOW-WORMS (Male and Female).
The glow-worm's radiation comes from some slow process of chemical change, and appears to act as an attraction to the opposite sex.

Professor Beebe, has been able to watch these fish through the windows of his special diving chamber, the " bathysphere," as they swim half a mile below the surface of the sea in what would be complete darkness, but for the lights which these fish carry. There are fish with practically every shade of light, from red to blue, and some carry patterns of several colours. Some squids also are luminescent, and one of them has the strange power of squirting out a luminous fluid into the water surrounding it. This is the exact opposite of the octopus' habit of squirting " ink."

Sometimes the sea itself appears luminous although the light comes, not from the water itself, but from minute living organisms feeding in it. Altogether, as many as forty different orders of living creatures contain light-producing species. Still keeping to the sea, there are luminous shrimps and also sea worms, as well as fish and squids. Jelly-fish, too, may carry their own illumination.

On land, fireflies and glow-worms are the best-known examples. Both of these, in spite of their names, are really beetles. Some species even go so far as to lay eggs which, like the adult " fly," will shine in the dark. As well as these, there are luminescent earthworms and even centipedes. It is a strange sensation to pick up such a creature from the mud of an English lane, and even stranger to find some of its light-giving fluid sticking to one's fingers, so that these, too, will glow in the darkness.

In addition, some bacteria are luminescent, and so also are some fungi. The case of the bacteria is rather curious. Sometimes they seem to live on friendly terms with their animal host, making him luminous, but doing him no harm. It has, in fact, been suggested that a large proportion of living " phosphorescence " is due to a partnership of this kind. But in other cases, these light-giving bacteria are responsible for disease. Some species of sand-fleas and of shrimps suffer from a fatal disease of this kind, although, as has already been mentioned, there are other shrimps which are luminescent on their own.

[*W. S. Berridge.*
Jelly-fish may carry their own illumination.

Light-giving fungi are responsible for the glow which is sometimes to be seen from decaying wood. Light may be given out either by fungus of the fine thread-like kind, which literally penetrates through and through the wood in which it grows, or by the more familiar type of fungus which grows on its own.

One of the biggest puzzles about these natural examples of " phosphorescence " is to know what purpose this strange power of giving out light can serve. In some cases, such as some of the fish which have been mentioned, it is natural to suppose that it is an advantage to the fish to carry its own headlamps. In the case of the fireflies, it appears that the light acts as an attraction to the opposite sex. But neither of these explanations can be applied to the smallest of these light-producing creatures—the minute sea animals already mentioned, or the still more minute bacteria. In either case, the bearers of the light are too primitive to be able to make any use of it. They have not got eyes, or for that matter a nervous system such as we have. Therefore, in such cases as these, scientists can only imagine that the " phosphorescence " is more or less of an accident. Chemicals are produced in the bacteria which serve some other useful purpose, and it is a mere chance that light, of whatever colour, is also provided.

CREATURES OF THE DEEP.

Luring a giant Oarfish to its doom. But for the lights—practically every shade from red to blue—carried by these fish, there would be complete darkness half a mile below the surface of the sea.

THE ANTENNÆ OF A MALE EMPEROR MOTH (MAGNIFIED). [H. Bastin.

INSECT "WIRELESS"

MANY insects can communicate with one another over quite long distances. When one thinks of the sizes of insects compared with the size of a man, a few feet or yards is a long distance. Also, they have no mechanical means like drums, loud-speakers, microphones, or telephones to assist them, such as we have. They use only their senses of hearing and smell. To us this seems very strange, but to most insects their sense of smell conveys much more than their sight, which is not highly developed like ours.

Insects respond only to a limited number of sounds directly connected with their lives; for example, the hum produced by the wings of a female mosquito as she flies past causes the hairs on the antennæ or "feelers" of the male mosquito to twitch rapidly. Those insects which make sounds by scraping one part of the body against another, crickets, grasshoppers and "singing" cicadas, for example, can hear the noises from afar and so are led to one another. The "ears" of insects may be on the first legs below the knee joints or on the abdomen or on the antennæ. Certain butterflies attract the attention of their mates by curious loud clicking, rattling, or whistling noises. If one ant of a colony gets into difficulties, it can send out a message for help to its fellows by making scraping noises, and they rush to its assistance.

16

[*Dr. Graf Zedtwitz.*

The long and extremely sensitive antennæ of this remarkable insect are used to find its mate. Notice, also, the big eyes.

Or, if an exploring ant finds a quantity of food, the good news is passed on in the same way, and numbers of its comrades come hurrying along.

By means of their sense of smell, insects are able to find each other over much longer distances, even up to a distance of a few miles. Generally, we cannot smell the various scents which they give off, and we certainly cannot distinguish between one kind of ant and another, or between different kinds of bees and wasps by smell alone. If a female Oak Eggar moth which has just emerged from a chrysalis is placed in a small cage out of doors or even in a room in a house, soon numbers of male Oak Eggar moths will fly to her, though none may have been seen in the neighbourhood for some time beforehand. Male moths have been known to come from a distance of two to three miles. Think how keen the male moths' sense of smell must be ! We could not smell a female Oak Eggar moth from even a couple of feet away. The smelling organs which receive the scent from such long distances are found chiefly in the antennæ. These are often branched and feathery and are very sensitive indeed. They act like two long noses which can be turned in all directions to catch the various scents. The antennæ of male insects are frequently more elaborate and more sensitive than those of the females, since it is the males which have to seek out their mates. In the male or drone bee about 60,000 sensitive spots occur in the antennæ, in the worker bee 12,000, and in the queen bee only between 4,000 and 6,000.

[*H. Bastin.*

The huge laminated antennæ of a Mexican Chafer Beetle.

[B.N.A.
A wonderful photograph, obtained by a Swiss photographer, of
that mysterious phenomenon, the spectre of the Brocken.

THE SPECTRE OF THE BROCKEN

FROM the Brocken Mountain in Germany, and sometimes from
other peaks, the walker, when the sun is low in the sky, may
see a giant figure striding the clouds a little below him and surrounded
by a complete rainbow in the form of a circle—something which, in
itself, can never be seen at ground level. Those who have seen the
spectre say that they never expect to see anything more wonderful.

This phenomenon is caused by conditions very similar to those
that produce an ordinary rainbow. The sun's rays are reflected and
spread out by minute droplets of water in the morning or evening
mist. Each of the different colours of which sunlight is made up are
separated from the others inside the water droplets. The separation
of the different colours is due to the fact that violet light, on passing
from air into water, is deviated from its course to a greater extent than
is red light.

The rainbow of the Brocken is circular because, when the observer
is standing high up on the mountain, the whole of the rainbow can be
seen ; and just as a second bow can sometimes be seen outside the
main bow, but with the colours in the reverse order, so on the Brocken
the giant spectre may sometimes be seen surrounded by two distinct
circles of coloured light.

And the spectre itself, as may perhaps have been guessed, is
nothing more than the watcher's own shadow, much enlarged through
the bending of the sun's rays.

The " spectre " is not necessarily confined to the Brocken Mountain.
It has, for example, been seen on the Coulins of Skye.

GLASS STRONG ENOUGH TO CARRY AN ELEPHANT

IF you were walking down the street and suddenly saw an elephant standing on a large sheet of glass, you would no doubt rub your eyes in astonishment. Yet this is not impossible.

And in the picture you will actually see an elephant standing on a sheet of plate glass ; and an attempt was lately made to *sling* an elephant from a sheet of glass, but when the elephant showed signs of disliking the idea, a lorry carrying a number of men was used instead. The load was just as great, probably greater.

Until only a few years ago, glass was regarded as being necessarily quite fragile, and it was said that " people who lived in glass houses should not throw stones." Now, thanks to the persistent researches of scientists, glass can be made into a vastly different product. A form of heat treatment can be applied to give it strength—a process similar to some by which metals are made hard.

Such glass is of the special type known as " Armourplate." This is genuinely glass, and transparent like any other ; but it has greatly increased strength and will stand violent shocks without breaking. Even when it is twisted back and forth, through about fifteen degrees, it will not snap. It can also be heated up to 480 degrees Fahrenheit —at which heat tin would be molten—and even at this temperature cold water can be dropped on the glass without breaking it, an extraordinary performance when it is remembered how easily an ordinary wineglass breaks when held under a tap that is too hot. It is because of this power to withstand large differences in temperature between one surface and the other that such glass can be used in oven doors, in fire screens, and for other purposes of a similar nature.

However, the fact remains that the most spectacular quality of " Armourplate " glass is its strength. A quarter-inch sheet is enough to support a weight of two hundredweight, and even the " elephant test " was made with a sheet no more than an inch thick. And if this kind of glass does break, then it shatters into minute fragments which it is claimed are too small to cause any injury.

Because of its strength, and its power of withstanding sudden shocks, this glass is used in such places as portholes, where it will stand up to very much rougher treatment than will ordinary glass.

AN ELEPHANT WEIGHING SEVERAL TONS STANDING ON A SHEET
OF PLATE GLASS.

A somewhat similar glass is now used in the observation cars of railways.

Glass floors, glass bricks, and glass fireplaces are some of the other achievements of modern glassmakers ; so that, if anyone wanted to, it would almost be possible to build an all-glass house, and one, moreover, which would not be unduly vulnerable to attack by stones. It is even claimed that by using coloured glass, flies can, to a large extent, be kept away from the larder. Flies, it has been found, dislike coloured light, especially red and yellow, so that by using window glass of either of these two colours flies can be driven away. This discovery has been put to practical use in food factories.

WHAT MAKES YOUR HAIR STAND ON END?

THERE are glands hidden away inside the body, which make your hair stand on end. They are members of an important group of glands, each of which makes one or more different chemicals which they pass out into the blood stream, and through these chemicals control very many of the body's activities. These particular glands, the adrenal glands near the kidneys, make the chemical " adrenin." Its job is to mobilise the body for any special physical effort, as, for example, under natural conditions, in preparation for a fight. So two of the things which adrenin does are directed towards frightening your opponent. It makes the hair stand on end ; and enlarges the pupils of the eyes, which also helps to give a man a terrifying appearance. However, that is only what may be called window-dressing, and adrenin has a number of other effects which are more seriously designed to increase efficiency. It speeds up the muscles of the heart, so increasing the supply of oxygen to the muscles, and also helps the blood to flow throughout the body. It slows down the process of digestion, because in time of emergency that is so much wasted effort. And, finally, it urges the sweat glands to action. All of these last effects are of obvious importance in any form of serious effort, so that adrenin is a good friend to the athlete. This does not mean, however, that it would be wise to take an extra supply before any form of athletic contest. The adrenal glands provide as much as it is good for the body to be given, the necessary supply having presumably been adjusted to our needs during the slow course of evolution.

"WHAT'S THAT?"

EYES OF MANY KINDS

ALTHOUGH animals may appear to be viewing things much as we do, yet their outlook on life may be something entirely different. Their vision is often so much supplemented by their senses of smell and hearing, that it sometimes becomes almost a negligible factor.

An otter moving in an open field may remain unseen by the otter hounds that hunt it, if the hounds have not crossed the track of its scent. With greyhounds, though, it would be very different. They hunt the hare purely by sight, and will course the " electric hare," which, of course, has no scent.

With both the hare and the rabbit sight holds first place. The first action of a startled rabbit is to drop its ears flat on to its body, and crouch low, while its eyes bulge out to large proportions. Their angle of sight can then encircle the whole body. If still suspicious, its next move is to erect its ears to listen.

Birds, likewise, show similar variations in their powers of vision. There is the kestrel that poises itself high in the air on rapidly-vibrating wings while carefully searching the ground with its telescopic eyes for a field-vole, or even a beetle, moving amongst the grasses. Then it falls like a bolt on its unsuspecting victim. During that downward swoop the kestrel's eyes have changed from telescopic to normal, and, perhaps to microscopic vision.

In contrast to that marvellous eye function we may instance the numerous thrushes and other

[*H. Bastin.*

THE STALK-EYED CRAB.

song birds we see killed on the roads by motor traffic. These birds, with their lateral or monocular vision, seem entirely unable to estimate distance and oncoming speed. The owls, with frontal vision, also

Mondiale]   [*W. S. Berridge.*

THE FOUR-EYED FISH (*Anableps tetropthalmus*).

the eagles and hawks, whose eyes nearly approach it, are experts at judging distance.

Fishes, too, have lateral vision, but there again it is much modified. There are some small

fishes, found in estuaries of tropical America, known as Double-Eyes (*Anableps*), which have eyes divided into upper and lower halves. The upper lenses are biconvex, and the lower spheroidal. As the fish swim at the water surface, their eyes are thus adapted for both air and water vision.

Turning to the invertebrate animals, we find there eyes of many kinds. The Great Kraken marine monster, a kind of cuttle-fish, or squid, with a body about ten feet in length bearing eight arms each about six feet long, and two of over forty feet, completes

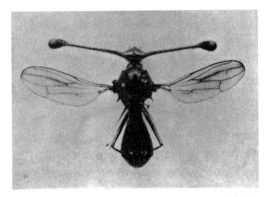

[*H. Bastin.*

A STALK-EYED FLY OF EAST AFRICA.

its fearsome " make-up " with eyes of soup-plate proportions.

Against these large eyes, always associated with depths and darkness, there are the crabs with small periscope-like eyes elevated on stalks. The garden snail is also provided with similar elevated eyes, but of a much more primitive type. The snail is so short-sighted that you have nearly to touch one of its eyes before it is suddenly retracted into the feeler. Even then, the eye on the tip of the opposite feeler remains projected and knows nothing of what has happened on the other side.

Finally, there are the compound eyes of insects. Eyes composed of thousands of lenses, each one of which receives an image. That, however, does not necessarily mean that the insects see that number of objects. We look at an object with our two eyes, yet only one image is recorded on our brain. It may be the same with insects.

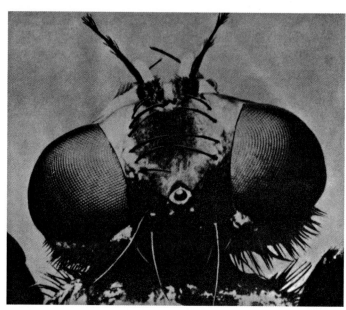

[E.N.A.

HEAD OF THE COMMON HOUSE FLY, GREATLY MAGNIFIED AND SHOWING THE EYES WITH MANY FACETS.

We know, however, that some insects can view colours at the ultra-violet end of the spectrum which the human eye has never yet seen, and that they fail on the red side. To a bee red is black, or darkness —just as it is to a photographic plate. Strange to relate, the photographic plate, like the bee's eyes, can receive the ultra-violet rays.

The little whirligig beetle, often seen in groups on the surface of a pool, has its compound eyes divided into upper and lower halves for air and water vision, just like those of the double-eyed fishes. It would be interesting to see those surface-feeding fishes trying to capture these beetles—playing their own game.

IT *DOES* RAIN FROGS AND FISHES

A BABY FROG,
with the remains of the tail it had as a tadpole.

IN a well-known story, Turi the Lapp told of toads that fell in hundreds from the sky. This was no novelist's romance. There have been more than seventy reports in the past 1,600 years of showers of frogs or fishes coming down from the clouds. The explanation is that high winds, particularly whirlwinds, pick up water in the form of waterspouts and with it carry up whatever life the water may contain. Two of the latest of such stories come from America. On May 15th, 1900, a heavy downpour of rain on Rhode Island brought down so many living perch and " bullpouts " that children were able to gather them by the pailful and sell them. Similarly on May 18th, 1928, a shower of hundreds of fishes fell on a farm in North Carolina.

The farm was three-quarters of a mile from the nearest stream and, since there were very few fish to be found in this stream, the " shower " must have been carried from some greater distance. The earliest story of the kind dates from 300 A.D., and America is far from having a monopoly of such events—except, perhaps during the present century. Even Great Britain, with its much smaller area, can claim some seventeen recorded instances of showers of fishes. In fact, since the total number of " fish showers " for the whole of the rest of Europe is no more than sixteen, it looks as though Britain must be one of the likeliest countries for fish to fall from the sky. But to wait for this to happen would be a poor way of earning a living, for, as might be expected, the fish when they come are generally small.

Photos by]   [*Ewing Galloway, N.Y.*
A YOUNG TADPOLE.

25

DISTANCES, SPEEDS AND NUMBERS UNBELIEVABLE

OUR home, the planet Earth weighing 6,000 trillion tons, is just one of eight other similar bodies and twenty odd minor bodies called moons which revolve round a central sun seven hundred times heavier than all of them put together. All these make up what is called a solar system—*our* solar system, whose size is such that, whereas a cruise round the world in a luxury liner takes about two months and costs about £200, a similar cruise round the solar system would occupy *about two thousand life-times and cost about £150 million sterling*. Yet

this entire system is a mere speck in a forgotten little nook of the Universe. The sun, so bright and hot, and a million times bigger than the Earth, is itself but one very ordinary member of a colossal community of stars called the *Galaxy* or

Photo]   [*Yerkes Observatory, Chicago.*
The great nebula of Andromeda as photographed with the two-feet reflector of the Yerkes Observatory. An exposure of four hours was given.

Galactic System, numbering more than 100,000 million at least and probably twice as many.

The shape of the galaxy is a remarkable cartwheel (the great astronomer Herschel likened it to a great grindstone) and it is rotating like a grindstone or cartwheel. The sun, of course, partakes of this sublime rotatory motion and, being situated far nearer to the centre than to the rim, describes an orbit far smaller than the stars nearer the outside or those of the Milky Way, which form the rim. *Yet at* 200 *miles a second it takes the Sun not less than two million centuries to get round once*—to complete a single lap of his mighty, non-stop marathon round the hub of the galactic system.

DISTANCES, SPEEDS AND NUMBERS UNBELIEVABLE

The Sun is only the nearest star—the star of day, *our* star he may be called. He shines with a light brighter than the combined light of 3000,000,000,000,000,000,000,000,000 candles (3,000 quadrillion or 3,000 million million million million). Yet plenty of stars in the galaxy are a hundred times brighter than he is. One called *S. Doradus* is actually 300,000 times *brighter*. The face of Old Sol is five times hotter than molten metal in a Bessemer steel furnace. Yet the faces of all blue, blue-white, and white stars are much hotter, while only two colours of stars are cooler, the red and orange. A few stars are a million times smaller than the Sun, the white dwarfs for instance, but there are many a thousand times larger. One of the biggest, called *Betelgeux, is twenty-five million times bigger ;* 25 million Suns could be packed inside it. This giant red star is to be found in the best-known of all groups of stars—the constellation *Orion,* and *it consists of material a thousand times lighter than the very air we breathe.* As Sir Arthur Eddington says, we " should call it a vacuum were it not contrasted with the much greater vacuosity of surrounding space." On the other hand, most of the white dwarf stars consist of stuff so compact and dense that if you had a pair of shoes made from it, they would weigh—*about* 500 *tons.* The Sun radiates fifty horse-power of energy from every square inch of its surface, but the average white dwarf radiates two hundred and fifty horse-power per square inch— five times as much. One

By courtesy of the Director, Lowell Observatory, Arizona, U.S.A.
HALLEY'S COMET.
The photograph was taken at the Lowell Observatory, Arizona, in 1910. The bright central head of a comet consists of a cluster of lumps of stone or iron, and is at times thousands of miles in width. These lumps contain gas. When a comet approaches the sun, the gas is drawn out by the heat and then flows in a long stream, called the tail. The Earth passed through the edge of the tail of Halley's comet on May 19th, 1910. This famous comet returns about every 75 years.

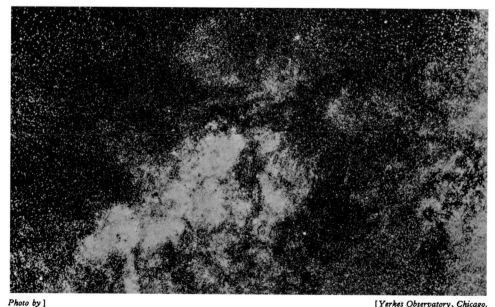

Photo by]   [*Yerkes Observatory, Chicago.*
PART OF THE MILKY WAY.
Every white dot is a sun, probably much larger and brighter than our sun.

very hot star called *Plaskett's Star*, however, radiates no less than twenty-five thousand horse-power per square inch. Thus a single square inch of this star's surface gives off *enough energy to keep the " Queen Mary " always going at full steam ahead*, day and night, without stopping.

Not all stars shine with a steady light as does the Sun. Large numbers are known as " variables," since their brightness varies from time to time. They are winking, flickering lights like a torch in a breeze. In some cases it is as if someone were shovelling coal on to the stellar fire at perfectly regular intervals. The *Cepheid* variables are renowned for the perfect punctuality of their light fluctuations, which can be predicted with mathematical accuracy. None of these stars can possibly be attended by life-bearing planets. Any worlds like ours which may revolve round them could not possibly be inhabited *for many variable stars double their light and heat in the short space of a day or two*, while some are as much as fifty fold brighter at one time than at another. *Mira Ceti, for instance, increases in brightness one thousand times in five months.* If the Sun—our star—behaved anything like this, the Earth would be alternately burnt to cinders and then frozen hard.

DISTANCES, SPEEDS AND NUMBERS UNBELIEVABLE

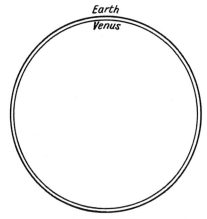

Earth
Venus

Venus and the Earth differ in size less than these two circles. Venus is the smaller.

With a starry population of probably 200,000,000,000, the Galactic System should have an acute over-crowding problem if anybody should. Yet there is none at all, quite the reverse in fact. *Half-a-dozen little fish, sprats or sardines, in the whole Atlantic Ocean would not be more utterly alone and free to roam than is the solar system in the Galaxy.* The elbow room given to the celestial household surpasses in immensity its total population. The nearest star is about twenty-five millions of millions of miles away. The fastest, non-stop aeroplane would thus need 7,000,000 *years to fly from the Sun to the Sun's next-door neighbour in space—the nearest star.*

One of the most famous of celestial sights is the great globular cluster of stars in the constellation *Hercules*, officially numbered M13 in the astronomers' star catalogue. *This superb cluster contains over 100,000 stars, each brighter and bigger than the Sun,* besides several times this number of smaller fainter ones. They are all in rapid motion together like a mammoth flock of starry swallows migrating to another part of the heavens. In all, *M13 is no less than two and a half million times more brilliant than Old Sol.* Yet so immeasurably remote is it, that good eyes and good seeing conditions are necessary to see it at all without optical assistance. *It is so far away that a ray of light, leaving it 33,000 years ago, will now be just reaching*

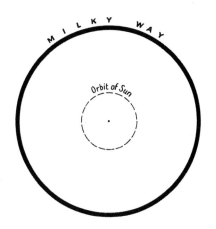

THE GALACTIC SYSTEM.

The small circle represents the Sun's orbit, which it takes 200 million years to traverse once. The huge outer cartwheel of stars forms the Galaxy. This diagram would have to be enlarged to the size of North America before a body proportionally so small as the Sun could be represented to scale by the tiniest dot.

By courtesy of]   [*The Carnegie Institute, Washington.*

RELATIVE SIZES OF THE SUN AND PLANETS.

Upper : A segment of the Sun in scale with the Planets.

Lower (left to right): Mercury, Venus, Earth and Moon, Mars, Jupiter, Saturn, Uranus, Neptune and Pluto.

the Earth. Another wonderful object, best seen in the southern hemisphere, is the *Lesser Magellanic Cloud,* which contains several million suns, *half a million of them brighter than Sirius, the Dog Star, which in turn is itself twenty-six times brighter than our Sun.* To the naked eye, even this gorgeous blaze of glory shows as nothing better than an insignificant little smudge of milky light on the black night sky, for its light takes 95,000 years to reach us, travelling night and day at 186,000 miles a second. Compared with this, a cruise round our solar system costing £150 million, becomes a mere constitutional.

Until not so long since, men thought that the Galaxy was, and must be, all the Universe. And no wonder, considering its awesome dimensions and bewildering profusion of blazing, moving, spinning orbs. But this idea was an error due purely to their puny faculties and appliances. More powerful instruments, the 100-inch telescope in particular, quickly proved them wrong. The great mirror pierced through and beyond the Milky Way, the outer rim and frontier of our star system, and showed at unbelievable distances out in the depths of cosmic space, other systems definitely comparable with ours—the spiral nebulæ, sometimes termed just " spirals " for short. *The Galaxy became only one among two million.* It was found to be no more the whole Universe than London is the whole Earth. The nearest " spiral " is 850,000 light years* away—200,000 times further away than the nearest star, which in turn is itself a million times further away than the nearest planet, *Venus.* Since the light by which we see it takes this time to reach us, any of the spiral nebulæ may have long vanished from the sky without us knowing about it. *Even the nearest one would have to be dead and buried* (its light extinguished) *for nearly a million years before news of its decease could reach us on the wings of light.* We should then be told by the messengers of light FAILING TO ARRIVE. The largest of the spirals, the *Great Nebula in Andromeda,* is so vast that the Earth in her orbit travelling at eighteen miles a second would need five million centuries to cross from one side of it to the other. It consists of gaseous material so inconceivably light and tenuous that *a boy could easily balance on his little finger, a lump as big as the Matterhorn.* This notwithstanding, it contains enough matter to make 3,000 million Suns as big as ours. The absurd lightness of the Great Nebula is due to the fact that, whereas in the emptiest vacuum tube which men can produce there are still left 500,000 million molecules to the cubic inch, in the Andromeda Nebula *there are only two or three to the cubic inch.* As previously mentioned, the star Betelgeux is made of flimsy stuff 1,000 times lighter than air, but most of the spirals are made of gases 1,000 *million times lighter than this again.* Naturally, they are most transparent, and astronomers are usually able to see clearly into and through them to the extent of thousands of millions of miles. While not so vast as our nebula or galaxy, the spirals are much too large and distinctive to be classed as anything less grand than galaxies or " island universes " of stars. Many are cartwheel shaped and all rotate like our own system. Some are as flat as pancakes—the result of very fast rotation. Their average distance from each other is about two million light years,* *about 11 million million million miles* (or 11 followed by 18 zeros). The most remarkable thing about them, however, is that they are mostly in headlong flight *away from us.* Examined in a spectroscope, the light from a distant object becomes redder than usual if the object is receding, and bluer than usual if it is coming towards us, the amount of extra-colouring depending chiefly upon the speed of the moving object. Now the light from nearly all of the great island universes is enormously redder than it should be, *far redder in fact than is the light from any other celestial objects.* Which indicates enormous velocities of recession or retreat, ranging from scores to thousands of miles a second. Still more startling, perhaps, is the fact that in many instances, *the rate of retreat varies in exact ratio to the distance.* The farther they are away from us the faster do they appear to fly away from us. At present, the most remote nebula, at a distance of 400 million light years or so, is apparently stampeding from the Earth at 40,000 miles a second. Moreover, the great star systems are not only, on present evidence, running away from us, *they are also running just as hard away from each other.* Here we have the starting point of the sensational current doctrine of the expanding universe, the possibility or rather the inevitability of which was hinted at in the equally famous *Theory of Relativity*. If the fragments of the Universe (the galaxies or spirals) are all opening out and flying apart like the fragments of a bursting shell on a battlefield, then clearly, the Universe is expanding. According to this now widely-accepted theory of the expanding universe, the nebulæ are not moving *through* space but *with* space. Ordinary brains like ours, of course, cannot comprehend this—we cannot possibly imagine how empty space can expand, but it will help if we compare the spirals to straws in a stream

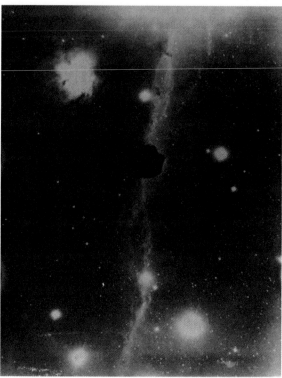

By courtesy of]   [*Mount Wilson Observatory.*

A NEBULA SOUTH OF ZETA ORIONIS.
About ten million Nebulæ are visible in the 100-inch Mount Wilson telescope. The majority are so huge as to be incomprehensible to the human mind. They are formed of incandescent gaseous matter and appear as dim, luminous, cloud-like areas in the sky.

or wisps of cloud. Wisps of cloud show which way the currents of air are moving, they are borne along *by* them and *with* them. Wisps of gas on the astronomical scale, i.e. nebulæ, *show which way the currents of space are flowing;* they are being swept along by them and with them. The speeds of the retreating spirals, proportional to their distances from us, indicate that cosmic space is expanding evenly and equally in all directions at once, something after the fashion of the skin of a toy balloon while being inflated. If the speeds be anything like what they seem to be, then it would be more accurate to speak of the *exploding* universe, *for they are hundreds of times swifter than any speed dynamite or gunpowder can produce by explosion.*

There is a doubt, however, as to whether the nebula speeds are really as high as at first thought. Other things besides mere retreat can produce a reddening of rays, only one important instance of which can be given here. It is suspected that where such vast distances as those of the spirals are concerned, *even light itself begins to tire a little* and consequently redden as its vibrations are slowed down. Hardly any scientists believe that these other causes produce ALL the observed reddening of the light from the spirals. On the contrary, a great majority are convinced that the spirals really are receding and scattering at enormous speeds, and that much, if not most, of their exceedingly reddened light is due to this recession. Professor Milne said that to him, the expansion of the Universe was the most natural thing in the world, for the word firmament is found in Genesis, *and is the Hebrew for expansion.* In any case, the behaviour of these incredibly remote spiral universes is being most closely studied, for sooner or later it will surely provide a clue to the origin, nature, and destiny of the whole material creation. Two million spirals are already known. The new 200-inch telescope now in course of construction, is expected to reveal perhaps fifteen million more. Even with the super 200-inch mirror, we shall still probably be able to see round only a one-millionth part of the total volume of space there is in the Universe. If all the stars in the sky were grains of sand, *there would be enough of them at a low estimate to cover all Wales a quarter of a mile deep.* And they are all wasting away at an appalling, unimaginable rate. They are able to go on blazing and shining solely by means of a colossal, continuous sacrifice of their material substance—their body. The Sun—our star—is losing four million tons a second, day and night, year by year. Some stars lose 10,000 times as much. Thus the substance of the Universe is dissolving and disappearing into radiation at an undreamed of rate, faster than anything we can think. *Trillions, aye quadrillions of tons of it melt with every tick of the clock.* The size of the Universe increases, expands, by millions of miles a minute. Over 99 per cent. of the Universe consists of what we call empty space, sheer emptiness. Yet it is ever and always becoming emptier still.

A RIVER OF LOGS

WHEN we read our morning paper, we should think sometimes of all the many people who have helped to make it. We shall see what a number of people have been busy upon it. To find some of them we should have to travel over the seas to Canada. There, in the woods, are men who cut down the trees, and take down the logs to the river. But what have trees to do with the newspaper ? A very great deal ; for it is out of the wood-pulp made from trees that the paper is manufactured. Paper is made from other things as well : from linen and cotton rags, and from certain kinds of grass ; but for the enormous stores of paper required by our great dailies and other journals, there is need of this other supply which the lumber-men provide for us in the forests of the West.

But how are the logs carried down to the mills where they are crushed into pulp ? At certain times of the year, if we lived in Canada, we should see a river which looked exactly as if it were made of logs.

[*Dorien Leigh.*

BLASTING A LOG JAM ON A RIVER IN NORTHERN QUEBEC.

A RIVER OF LOGS

The current carries them down. Sometimes there is a complete jam; and then it is necessary to blast the fixed mass which has formed, and set the logs in motion again. The river serves both as a goods train and a motor-van. After the long journey is over the logs are taken out of the river and crushed in the mill. The pulp is brought to the machines, and night and day the mighty engines are at work, all preparing the paper for us. But we should not forget those lonely lumber-men far away in the forests, who cut down the trees, which give us the pulp, which gives us the paper, which gives us the news.

By courtesy of]   [Caterpillar Tractor Co.
LUMBERMEN FELLING A GIANT WHITE PINE TREE.

A REMARKABLE ANT-HILL IN CENTRAL AUSTRALIA.

Termite Ants' nests are composed of earth cemented with the insects' saliva, and frequently reach an astonishing size.

The attitude of the Tawny Frogmouth (*Podargus strigoides*) when alarmed. In this position it looks exactly like a broken branch.

Photos]   [Otto Webb.

The bird in its normal attitude on its flimsy nest of sticks in the Australian bush.

NATURE'S PROTECTION

Stick Insects, which are long and thin like twigs and closely resemble the shoots among which they sit.

BLUFF

INSECTS have many clever and varied ways of saving themselves from the host of enemies by which they are always surrounded. There are four main methods into which these ways of protection may be grouped.

The first is called the aggressive method, by which we mean that the insects fight their enemies with poison stings, like Wasps and Bees ; with powerful jaws, like Soldier Ants ; with harmful gases, like Bombardier Beetles and Puss Moth Caterpillars.

The second method is by being unpleasant or dangerous to eat. Insects protected in this way usually advertise their nastiness by brilliantly-coloured bodies and wings so that their enemies may learn rapidly to recognise them and leave them alone. It is obviously an advantage to insects of this sort to warn their enemies that they are unfit to be eaten before the enemy attacks and injures them. Examples of such insects are Lady-bird Beetles, caterpillars of the Cinnabar and Buff-tip Moth, and hairy caterpillars of the Tiger Moth.

The third method is camouflage. By this we mean that insects which are good to eat escape their enemies by disguising themselves to look like a part of their surroundings. For instance, in Britain the Crimson Underwing

THE INDIAN LEAF BUTTERFLY.
Top : With wings spread.
Bottom : Resting on a twig with three leaves. Notice how closely the markings on the wings resemble the veining of the leaves.

Photos]   *[H. Bastin.*
THE GREEN-LEAF INSECT from CEYLON.

This insect is green to resemble the foliage it frequents, and it will be seen that the extensions on the legs imitate very closely the leaflets on the leaf-stalk.

Moth is conspicuous in flight and escapes its pursuers by settling on a tree trunk, when it seems to vanish, for it then very closely resembles the bark of the tree. But it has only folded its wings, so hiding the crimson spots on the underwing. The pursuer is misled by its sudden disappearance and continues to search for a gaily-coloured insect. By the same trick the Buff-tip Moth when it rests on the ground, looks like a short broken end of twig and the Indian Leaf Butterfly on closing its wings becomes a perfect model of a leaf, even having markings to

An Orange-Tip Butterfly resting among the tiny massed flowers of the Cow Parsley.

A Red Underwing Moth. When at rest on the bark of a tree, it is almost unseen. (Two moths on stem.)

Photos]

[*H. Bastin and Dorien Leigh.*

Caterpillars of the Pine Beauty Moth resting among pine "needles," which they greatly resemble.

Buff-tip Moths resting among debris. Note their stick-like form.

WHERE ARE THEY?

[H. Bastin.

Eye-spots on a tropical butterfly. Either way up the insect has a remarkably ogre-like appearance.

look like leaf veins, and a leaf stalk. There are the Stick Insects, which are long and thin like twigs, and Leaf Insects, which are green, thin and flat like leaves. These and other examples of camouflage are illustrated and you can see from the pictures what excellent disguises they all are.

The fourth method is mimicry, which means that insects which are really good to eat are protected by their resemblance in colours and shapes to dangerous or unpleasant kinds, like those mentioned in the first and second groups. There are many examples of mimicry in Britain, but the disguises of the defenceless insects are so perfect that unless examined closely they would be mistaken for the kinds of insects which they mimic. There is a harmless moth, the Poplar Clear-wing, which we would all avoid, so well does it deceive us by its wonderful resemblance to the vicious stinging hornet. Not only moths, but many other kinds of insects imitate the various stinging ones. Examples of such are a fly called the Drone Fly, which mimics the Hive Bee, and a beetle which mimics the Humble Bee. In the tropics are found many brilliantly-coloured butterflies which are distasteful to birds and lizards, and other creatures which feed on insects. Mimics of these are common and have often misled collectors. Other insects bluff their enemies

[E.N.A.

The head of the larva of the Swallow-tail Butterfly (greatly magnified).

The huge " eyes " are only make-believe to terrify a foe. The real head is the small semi-circular segment at the bottom of the picture.

BLUFF

by suddenly changing their entire appearance from an attractive meal into something hideous and frightening, as do the caterpillars of the Puss and Lobster Moths.

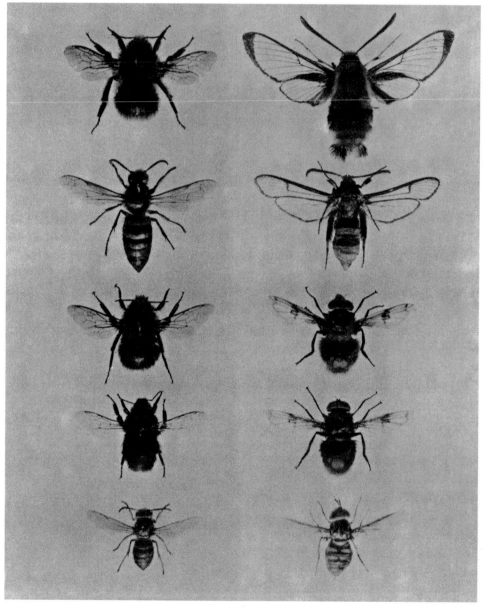

MIMICRY.

[*H. Bastin.*

Left : All stinging insects—bees and wasps.
Right : Harmless moths and flies which " mimic " the " warningly-coloured " stingers, and are so protected by their resemblance in colour and shape to the dangerous kinds.

42

A room at the Franklin Institute, Philadelphia, Pennsylvania, with apparently plain walls when viewed by *ordinary light*.

But switch on the *ultra-violet light* and these interesting mural paintings, by Mr. Charles Bittinger, are revealed. They show Franklin with his kite, and at his printing press. The artist used specially-prepared paints that included small quantities of certain substances which, under ultra-violet rays, " fluoresce," or become luminous and glow with various colours.

ULTRA-VIOLET " MAGIC."

SOME *VERY* CURIOUS PLANTS

THE Traveller's Tree (*Ravenala madagascariensis*) of Madagascar is a very peculiar-looking tree. It is a kind of palm closely related to the banana. The stem is about 12 feet high and it sends out leaves close together on opposite sides. The leaves themselves are about 6 feet long and are attached to stalks about 7 feet long and, as can be seen in the photograph, the whole thing resembles a gigantic fan. Water becomes stored up in the cup-like sheaths of the leaf stalks, and by cutting a hole, thirsty travellers can obtain the liquid. Hence the name Traveller's Tree.

Another strange tree, a relative of the myrtle, has large, hard, round fruits which look like the old-fashioned cannon-balls. Of course, it is called the Cannon-ball Tree (*Couroupita*). It is a native of tropical America and has large white or pinkish flowers which spring directly from the trunk and branches of the tree. The round, woody-shelled fruit contains a pleasant, sweet, but rather acid pulp.

The Candle Tree (*Parmentiera cerifera*) of Panama has four-foot long, candle-like fruits, which are very much liked by the cattle. It is said that the apple-like flavour of the " candles " can be tasted in the flesh of the animals which eat them. Not only do these fruits resemble candles in their shape and yellow colour, but they contain so much

[*E.N.A.*

A thirsty wayfarer drawing water from a Traveller's Palm (*Ravenala madagascariensis*) in Jamaica. Each of the long stalks holds upwards of a quart of clear, drinkable water.

A Candle Tree (*Parmentiera cerifera*), Ceylon, covered with its waxy-looking, candle-like fruits, some four feet long. They contain a considerable quantity of oil, and are used as cattle food.

[*E.N.A.*

fat that an oil which is used for illumination purposes can be obtained from them.

The Cow Tree or Milk Tree (*Brosimum Galactodendron*) is " milked " by the natives of the Cordilleras of Venezuela. When the stem is pierced, a large quantity of a sweet white fluid pours out. This looks exactly like milk and contains sugar and a fatty, waxy substance but has a slight odour of balsam. Curiously enough, another member of the same family as the Milk Tree provides the " bread " to go with the " milk." This is the Breadfruit Tree (*Artocarpus incisa*) of the South Sea islands, plants of which were carried by the ill-fated " Bounty " to be introduced into the West Indies. The fruit consists of a large, fleshy mass in which the seeds are embedded, the whole as large as a man's head. This is gathered before the seeds are ripe, sliced up like a loaf, and baked. It looks and tastes very like bread. The Breadfruit Tree was eventually taken to the West Indies and also introduced to other countries in the tropics. As a contrast to the edible products of this family (*Moraceae*), there is the poisonous milky juice which oozes out of incisions in the bark of the Upas Tree (*Antiaris toxicaria*) of Java, another member of the family. This milky juice solidifies into a kind of resin with which the Javanese used to poison their arrows and knives. The natives of Malabar make use of a relative of the Upas Tree in quite a different way. They cut the trunk and branches of this tree (*Antiaris saccifera*) into suitable lengths and then the extremely tough bark is removed in the form of sacks, a thin section of wood being left to form the bottom of the sack.

The Mangrove is found in India, China, South America and other parts of the tropics. It sends down roots from the branches, and spreading rapidly in this way it soon forms a dense thicket. These aerial roots quickly become stems and send out further roots; the whole tangle forms a huge sieve which retains the mud washed down by the river, with the result that large areas of water at the mouth of the river are turned into Mangrove swamp. Another peculiarity about the tree is that its seeds germinate before they leave the tree. When ripe, the seed sends out a long, pointed, root-like structure, which in about eight months' time grows to a length of two feet or more and an inch or two in width. The seedling is now so heavy that the slightest breath of wind will cause it to break away from the tree, and falling to the earth, the root will bore deeply into the mud and the young seedling will continue its growth.

A curious plant which grows in the southern United States is usually known as Spanish Moss (*Tillandsia usneoides*), although it really is not a moss at all but related to the pineapple. It hangs in great hair-like, silvery masses from the branches of trees to which it is attached by suckers. It is not a parasite; that is to say,

[E.N.A.

A Cannon-ball Tree (*Couroupita*), Trinidad, showing the curious fruit. It has large, white or pinkish flowers which spring directly from the trunk and branches.

it does not draw any nourishment from the tree on which it grows but just uses the tree as a support. Under the name of " vegetable hair," its fragile stems, after treatment, have been used to stuff mattresses and cushions.

The " manna " which fed the Israelites on their desert journey from Egypt to the Holy Land was once thought to be the sweet sap which exudes from the Tamarisk (*T. mannifera*). There seems to be no foundation for this view, however, and it is now regarded as certain that the " manna " was a kind of edible lichen. There are many different kinds of lichen, but most of them are very similar to the grey-green or yellowish crusts which we often see, on a country walk, covering the bark of old trees and the surface of rocks and stones. The Edible Lichen (*Lecanora esculenta*) of the Sinai Desert grows in thick crusts on stones and as it gets older pieces may get broken away from the main plant. These pieces become rolled up into balls and, being very light, they can be easily blown about by the wind. In the violent storms which rage in the desert rainy season, large numbers of these pieces of manna will be swept up and carried about hither and thither, finally collecting in heaps behind low bushes or rocks. Several pounds of the lichen can be collected by one man after such a storm and in time of famine the plant is used instead of corn, being ground, baked, and eaten as bread.

Another plant of the deserts of Egypt, Arabia and Syria is the Rose of Jericho, a tiny annual scarcely more than three or four inches high. When the dry season commences, the plant curls up into a ball, and its shallow roots being unable to hold, it is blown about by the wind. If it reaches a damp place, the plant will uncurl and produce flowers and seed. On this account it is sometimes called the Resurrection Plant. There is a legend which says that the Resurrection Plant blossomed at the birth of Christ, curled up at the Crucifixion, and opened again at Easter.

The Grass Tree (*Xanthorrhœa arborea*) of New South Wales is a very strange plant. It looks rather like an enormous mop with its thick mass of grass-like foliage growing from the top of a trunk about twenty feet high. The flowers appear in globular masses on long stalks, looking rather like drum-sticks as they stand up among the leaves. The Grass Tree belongs to the lily family (*Liliaceæ*), but from its appearance one would not suppose it to be even distantly related to the lilies which we grow in our gardens.

SOME *VERY* CURIOUS PLANTS

To the lily family also belongs the famous Dragon Tree (*Dracæna Draco*) of Orotava, in the Canary Islands. It is said to be 6,000 years old and probably the oldest plant in the world. The palm-like trunk is about 80 feet high and it is so thick that ten men holding hands can hardly reach round it. A red, resinous liquid oozes out of the trunk and is one of the many substances called "Dragon's Blood."

Spanish Moss (*Tillandsia usneoides*) draping the branches of a fine live Oak, on Avery's Island U.S.A. It is not really a moss, but is related to the pineapple, and is sometimes used to stuff mattresses and cushions.

About seventy years ago a most peculiar plant was discovered by Dr. Welwitsch, a botanical explorer, on the west coast of Africa. It consisted of a top-shaped stem which did not rise more than a foot above the surface of the ground, bearing two large flat leaves. The flat top of the stem was about three feet in diameter and the leaves, which were torn into many strips by the wind, were about 6 feet long and lying spread out on the earth. This extraordinary plant is related to the Conifers (the Pines, Firs, etc.), and its cones are produced on branches which arise round the margin of the stem. It is called *Welwitschia mirabilis*, after the man who first discovered it.

SOME *VERY* CURIOUS PLANTS

The Rose of Jericho, of the deserts of Egypt, Arabia and Syria dried up—

A peculiar-looking Australian tree is the Queensland Bottle Tree (*Sterculia rupestris*), which owes its name to the fact that its trunk is very much swollen at the middle, becoming narrower towards the top, looking very much like an enormous bottle. The tree is often as much as 50 feet high and 30 feet round the thickest part of the trunk. The wood of the tree is soft and spongy and it has a sugary, syrup-like sap. Men lost in the Australian bush have been able to keep alive without other food or water by eating the pulp of the Bottle Tree.

The Lace-bark Tree (*Lagetta lintearia*) of Jamaica furnishes a material which exactly resembles lace and is used for many similar purposes. The " lace " is really the inner bark of the tree and consists of interlacing fibres. The material is made into collars, into ropes, and fibre whips, and it can be washed with soap just as ordinary lace is. Charles II is said to have had a cravat made of the " lace " of the Lace-bark Tree.

A tree which provides butter, candles, lamp oil, an intoxicating drink, a lawn manure, and food for natives, grows in Bengal. It is the Mahua or Butter Tree (*Bassia latifolia*). The oil from which the butter and candles are made is extracted from the seeds of the tree and the residue is made into the lawn-dressing. The flowers are almost as useful as the seeds. A spirit is distilled from them which is made into a native drink and at one time the natives used to live on food made from the cooked flowers for several months in the year.

The False Dittany (*Dictamnus Fraxinella*) is a plant

Photos]   *[H. Bastin.*
—and after treatment in water, growing freely. Legend says that this little plant blossomed at the birth of Christ, curled up at the Crucifixion, and opened again at Easter.

which is frequently grown in gardens, but few people know that it will burst into flame if a lighted match is held close to the flowers. Numerous oil glands on the flower stalks give off a large quantity of a highly

inflammable vapour, which, especially on a hot day, will burn with a blue flame when ignited.

High up in the Swiss Alps and in the Arctic regions the white mantle of snow is sometimes marred by large blood-red blotches. This is the so-called Red Snow, a minute plant which lives on the surface of the snow. It is a kind of alga (*Spharella nivalis*), and is related to the amethyst-coloured slime that appears on the surface of stagnant water. One would imagine that the alga would find nothing to feed it on the surface of snow, but it apparently subsists on fungous spores, plant seeds, and the remains of insects which eventually fall onto the snow.

The Jackfruit Tree (*Artocarpus integrifolia*) of Cey-

[E.N.A.
A Bottle Tree (*Sterculia rupestris*), Queensland.
Men lost in the Australian bush have been able to keep alive without food and water by eating the soft and spongy pulp of this peculiar tree.

lon is a near relative of the Breadfruit ; its fruits are very similar and they are eaten by the natives in the same way, but they are very much larger in size, often weighing as much as sixty or seventy pounds. The tree itself reaches a height of about thirty feet and the milky juice which exudes from wounds in the bark can be made into a very sticky bird-lime.

A NATIVE OF CEYLON GATHERING JACKFRUIT.

A Jackfruit weighs as much as sixty or seventy pounds, and is two or three times as large as the true Breadfruit.   It is, incidentally, of a much softer quality.

51

SALMON LEAPING A TWELVE-FOOT FALL.
Salmon always find their way back to the river where they themselves started life.

HOW DOES THE SALMON KNOW?

SALMON spend most of their life in the sea, eating herrings and other small fish, but when they are three and a half or four years old, they swim up rivers to find safe places for laying their eggs. They are generally helped by tides at the start of the journey, but further upstream they have to fight their way against strong currents, leap up weirs and rapids, and even give up feeding in order to reach shallow, fast-running water where they can lay their eggs. During this difficult journey they lose their beautiful silvery colour and graceful shape. Their skins turn reddish-brown and spotty, and their flesh becomes pale and watery. The male Salmon's front teeth also grow extra big and his snout grows out in front and the bottom half turns up into a big hook.

The eggs are generally laid on a gravel river bed, and the mother Salmon first digs a shallow trench with her tail to hold them. She lays only a few at a time, then covers them with some gravel and moves further upstream to lay the next lot. Altogether a large Salmon might lay about 30,000 eggs, taking a week or two to lay and hide the various batches.

Salmon are quite exhausted and very thin and weak at the end of spawning, and some die of starvation or injuries, or are caught by otters and poachers before they can get back to the sea. When they do manage the return journey, and have plenty to eat once more, they soon regain their silver colouring and proper shape, and they may come upstream two or three times more during their life-time of about nine years.

In the meantime the eggs, which are generally laid in the autumn, lie in the river bed all the winter, and if the water is very cold, they do not hatch for about five months. The babies are called salmon " fry," and have no need to look for food at first because there is so much yolk in the eggs that enough is left over to feed them for a month after they hatch. They carry this little sack of food growing under their throats, and do not venture out of the gravel until it is finished. Then they begin to swim about in shoals, catching little insect grubs and other morsels of food. While they are swimming in the river they are called " parr," and have dark purplish-green backs and bars down their sides. When they are about two years old, they are ready for the sea, and their skins become a clear silvery colour, so that they can safely live in clear sea water instead of a weedy river. They swim right out to sea and grow very fast, and soon begin to look like their parents ; but when the time comes for each new lot of Salmon to come up a river and spawn, *they always find their way back to the river where they themselves started life.*

How do they know ?

That is indeed one of the mysteries of nature at present beyond human understanding.

[*Dorien Leigh.*

A MIGHTY LEAP.
When three and a half or four years old, the fish swim up rivers to find safe places for laying their eggs. Upstream they have to fight their way against strong currents and leap up weirs and rapids.

FEELING BY "WIRELESS"

THE sense of feeling may sometimes mean that an animal sees, hears, or smells, quite apart from the mere sense of touch.

The earthworm, for example, which is entirely devoid of eyes,

Antennæ of a Beetle—like a string of beads.

will back hastily into its burrow at the sudden light from a flash-lamp. Its whole skin surface is light sensitive, and it just *feels* the light rays.

A snake, when in action, is continually darting out its tongue into space. It is practically certain that it is feeling sensory vibrations of some kind with that organ. Maybe it is listening to, or even smelling, a distant frog it is endeavouring to capture for its next meal ; or perhaps it is transmitting " wireless " calls to find a mate ; for there is accumulating evidence showing that animals are continually emitting vibrations of some kind.

Antennæ of a male Drinker Moth.

A newly-emerged female Emperor moth enclosed in a box, and taken out on the moors, will attract male moths from all directions for hours together while she remains unmated. Obviously, she has transmitted some message. It may be some subtle form of scent that she emits, but there is now much evidence to show that she

" broadcasts " for a mate, and that her radiations are received on the feathery feelers of the male moth, which probably act as " aerials," as their branches are clothed with numerous sensitive bristles and hairs.

Fishes, likewise, receive vibrations through the water. Most of them are seen to have a characteristic, more or less conspicuous, line on each side of the body, running from the head to the tail fin—the lateral line, as it is called. This lateral line bears external pores connected with a tube sunk beneath the skin. The tube is filled with mucus, in which are numerous nerve fibres. By means of this complex organ, the fish is able to feel vibrations in the water. It provides a sort of combined sense of hearing and touch, which enables the fish to avoid obstacles, and its fellows, as it darts about.

Homing pigeons have similar semi-circular canals in their ears, which also serve as directive organs. Feeling, therefore, may sometimes mean much more than actual touching.

BEAVERS.

Having webbed feet, the Beaver is a great swimmer and diver and spends most of its time in the water. They live in large colonies. In order to live in comfort and construct their peculiar dome-like lodges, they must have a large lake and deep water. It is to gain this object that the Beavers build a dam. They are wonderful craftsmen and cut the trees to fall just where they want them. Those that do not fall actually into the water, they roll in, or if they are at a distance from the water's edge, the Beavers frequently cut canals to the main stream and so float the trees down. When Beavers are at work building a dam, there is a continual crashing of trees, but strange to say, no Beaver ever gets hurt by a falling tree, so methodical and skilful are their operations. Our coloured picture shows the Beavers at work on a tree by the water's edge.

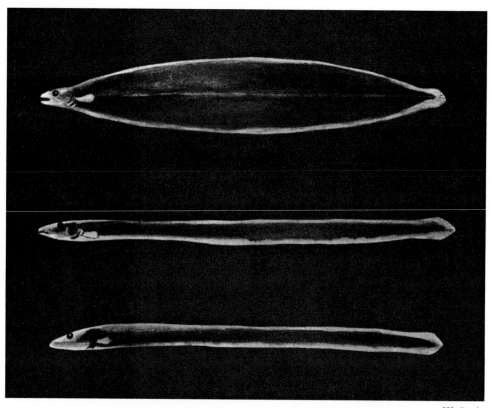

[*H. Bastin.*

Three stages in the development of the young eel. It will be seen that it is at first laterally compressed, like a " flat fish," and looks very much like a tiny, transparent willow leaf.

FOUR THOUSAND MILES!

MANY strange stories have been invented to explain where young eels come from, because no one has found any eel eggs or young in the rivers or ponds where big eels are quite common. Some people thought that when horses' hairs fell into water they grew into eels! Or that big eels rubbed themselves against rocks and stones, and the pieces they scraped off began to swim about as new baby eels!

Now we know that when eels have finished growing in the muddy beds of streams and canals and ponds all over Europe, their eyes become extra big, and their bodies turn silvery and black instead of mud-colour, and they swim down stream into the sea. If they have been living in a pond or canal, they wriggle out of the water and push their way overland to the nearest part of the west coast. They make this journey at night, when there is dew on the ground to keep them moist, and sometimes people mistake them for snakes and kill them. *All these eels then begin a long swim of three or four thousand miles right across the Atlantic*, and southwards, till they are in warm water near Bermuda. Here they lay as many as 10,000,000 eggs apiece, and very soon after, they die.

The eggs are light and transparent and float on the surface, where the baby eels hatch and begin swimming about. They look like tiny transparent willow leaves instead of being the shape of big eels.

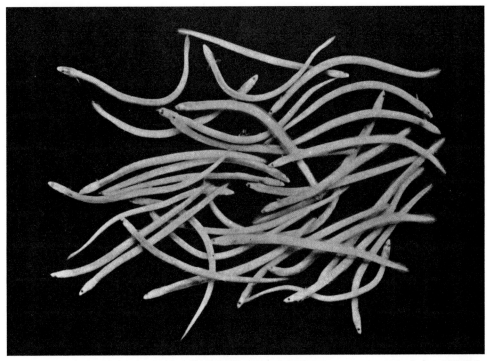

[*Mondiale.*

" GLASS EELS " OR ELVERS.
At this stage they must change their surroundings from salt to fresh water if they are to go on growing.
They move into river mouths and begin swimming upstream in shoals.

Gradually they move away from the Bermuda coast, and although they scatter, and thousands swim in every direction, most of them turn north-east, and in about two years the survivors have reached the coasts of Europe. By this time they are about three inches long, and still transparent and leaf-shaped, but they now stop growing, and even shrink a bit, then begin to change their shape until they look more like their parents, only colourless.

At this stage they are called " glass eels " or elvers, and must change their surroundings from salt to fresh water if they are to go on growing. They move into river mouths and begin swimming upstream

Eels live mostly on worms and other small water animals, but sometimes they catch water rats and even birds.

in such thick shoals, that sometimes three tons or more a day can be caught on their way up rivers like the Severn, that is, $5\frac{1}{2}$ millions of elvers! Such a procession upstream is called an "eel-fare" and may go on for days. Some of the elvers settle down in the upper reaches of the Severn or other rivers, but many of them wriggle over all sorts of barriers like weirs, and even travel overland to find other suitable feeding grounds. Here they settle down for the next seven or eight years, and sometimes grow to a length of four or five feet.

They eat mostly worms and other small water animals, but sometimes they catch water rats and birds, and one eel was found to have swallowed a pencil and a steel spring. Finally, they all recross the Atlantic, die near the American coast, after laying their millions of eggs to re-stock the rivers of Europe.

THE HERMIT CRAB TAKES HIS "DESIRABLE RESIDENCE," AND TWO LODGERS, WITH HIM.

The hermit crab inhabits a whelk shell, to which a sea-anemone, sometimes two even, is often attached. It is thought that the crab may benefit by the stinging power of the anemone, which gets carried about the sea floor, with increased chances of palatable food.

IT TOOK NO LESS THAN FIFTY-FIVE MEN TO BRING THIS ELEPHANT
TO A STOP. A RECENT TEST OF STRENGTH AT UYENO ZOO, TOKYO.

HOW STRONG IS IT?

A LARGE elephant, standing about eleven feet in height, may
weigh between six and seven tons. His carrying power, on a
short journey, may be eleven to twelve hundredweight, which, in
man-power, would require about thirty native carriers.

The load drawn by a powerful dray-horse may be two and a half
tons, to which about another ton has to be added for the weight of
the dray. Estimating the weight of the horse at fourteen hundredweight, it would be pulling a load equivalent to five times its own
weight. The pulling powers of a man, for a short distance pull, would
probably work out to similar proportions.

Strange to say, insects are proportionately much stronger than
human beings, horses and elephants.

From some experiments I made in harnessing insects to toy
trucks, I found that a blow-fly could pull a load one hundred and seventy
times its own weight. A ground beetle, six times the weight of the.

blow-fly, could pull only one hundred and eighty-two times its weight, which is but little more than that of the blow-fly.

The curious thing is, the smaller the insect, the greater is its proportional strength. An earwig, whose weight was just half that of the blow-fly, proved a veritable Hercules, for the load it pulled was five hundred and thirty times its own weight.

A BATTLE OF GIANTS.

THE FASTEST THING IN CREATION— A LIGHT YEAR

MILK is not sold by thimblefuls. Why? Because, of course, they are too small and unsuitable as units for measuring such a thing as milk. Similarly, then, as soon as men began a systematic search of the Universe, they found that even miles were far too small and unsuitable as units for measuring the distances of astronomical objects. The first new and bigger unit to be adopted was the distance between the Earth and the Sun—about 93 millions of miles. This also soon proved to be too small for most purposes. Next came the light year—the distance which light can travel in a year. A ray of light is the fastest thing in Creation, its normal velocity being 186,000 (approximately) miles a second in empty space. There are roughly $31\frac{1}{2}$ million seconds in a year, so that *a light year is equal to* 186,000 × $31\frac{1}{2}$ *million, or nearly* 6 *billion (million million) miles.*

When ready, as expected to be in 1940, the great new 200-inch telescope will be able to detect luminous objects nearly 1000 million light years away. This monster glass eye is over two feet thick, weighs

The sixteen-inch pilot telescope at California Institute of Technology that will be erected to scout the skies for the Giant 200-inch telescope on Palomar Mountain.

thirty tons, and will be nearly 750,000 (three-quarters of a million) times more powerful than the human eye. With its accessories and mountings it will weigh five hundred tons and cost about £1,000,000 sterling. If we use an ordinary tin funnel, many times more raindrops can be made to enter a bottle than without one. The wide mouth of the funnel overcomes the defect of the bottle's narrow neck. A telescope is built on the same principle. It is a sort of wide-mouthed light-funnel which catches a lot of light rays and sends them into our eyes. The power of a lens or mirror increases in proportion to the square of its diameter, or aperture, as this is generally called. Twice the aperture means not twice but four times the power. Four times the aperture brings sixteen times the power, and so on. The pupil of the human eye is about one-fifth of an inch in diameter. The diameter of the huge new mirror is 200 inches, or a thousandfold this. It ought, therefore, in theory, to be 1000 × 1000, a million times stronger than the human eye. In practice, however, it will amount to somewhat less. However excellent the workmanship, the actual magnification attained *always* falls short of the theoretical maximum for various technical reasons which hardly concern us here. To have an eye as far-seeing as the new telescope, a man would have to be a veritable Colossus.

[Wide World Photos.

Inspecting the " eye " of the giant 200-inch telescope. It weighs 30 tons and the bottom surface presents a honeycomb effect.

STRANGE EARS AND WHAT THEY HEAR

THE LARGE-EARED BAT.
It is probably able to hear the flying of a gnat at a considerable distance away.

WHEN we listen to birds singing, we must not imagine that we hear all their song.

Professor Allen, an American naturalist, has recently made some researches with recording apparatus showing that a wren uses one hundred and thirteen notes, of which we hear only five. It is the same with other birds. The sparrow runs off thirty-five different notes which, to us, are just a few erratic chirps.

Many animals are making sounds of which we know nothing. There is the long-eared bat with enormous ears, little inferior in length to its head and body, which enable it to hunt its prey by sound. This bat is probably able to hear the flying of a gnat at a considerable distance away; while the approach of a moth of medium size may sound to it like the rush of a locomotive does to us. Its voice is a very razor's edge of sound, so shrill that even some expert musicians fail to detect it. Its range of hearing commences on those octaves where the human sense fails.

Insects also have voices. We hear the shrill note of the male house-cricket when he calls his mate. When two male crickets are together, they chirp alternately, keeping almost regular time. If, however, one of them has its ears sealed with wax, they then chirp irregularly. Obviously, the one with the closed ears is not then hearing.

It is amazing in what strange places insects' ears are found. In the crickets and long-horned grasshoppers, they are situated just below the " knee " of

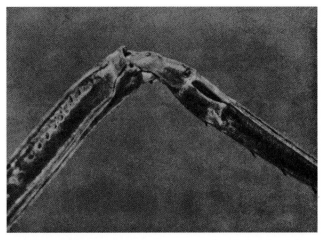

Leg of the Long-horned grasshopper, showing the ' ear ' opening below the knee.

each foreleg (as clearly shown in the first illustration on this page); while those of their relatives—those of the short-horned grasshopper— are found on each side of the first ring of the body, near the thorax (as shown in our second illustration on this page).

The gnat makes a shrill, piping note, but does not possess any real ears itself. It receives, however, sound vibrations with its feathery antennæ, or feelers, the hairs of which vibrate in unison with sounds that come within their range of " hearing." See also the article on INSECT "WIRELESS," page 19

When, as in the case of the gnat, ears do not exist as such, we have really approached the sense of feeling, and, under that heading, we will later consider the " hearing " or " feeling " of some other creatures, such as earthworms, snakes and fishes. The whole subject is one of amazing interest.

Photos]   *[H. Bastin.*
A Short-horned grasshopper, showing the ' ear ' opening just under the small wing-case. (Marked by arrow.)

TOO QUICK TO BE CAUGHT.
The bat's ears are so sensitive that it is almost impossible for an enemy to surprise it.

A novel raft. Sitting on a leaf of the *Victoria regia*, the Giant Royal Water Lily.

GIANTS

THE giants of the plant kingdom are the Sequoias (*Sequoia gigantea*) of California. These trees are the tallest in the world. Many of them are over 250 feet high, while the tallest is about 330 feet in height and with a girth of 75 feet at the base. If it grew in Trafalgar Square, it would tower nearly 200 feet above Nelson's Column and if the trunk were hollow, there would be room for one hundred and fifty children to stand inside. This tree, with ninety other giants, forms the Mammoth Grove of Calaveras County, so called because most of the trees are over 200 feet and three of them over 300 feet high. One of the largest of these trees was felled some time ago and a section of the trunk was sent to the Natural History Museum in London. Here the annual rings were counted and it was discovered that the tree was 1335 years old when it was cut down. It must have been a fairly large tree when Alfred was burning the cakes and the Danes were invading England.

The Eucalyptus trees of Australia, the tallest of which are about

275 feet high, are the nearest rivals to the Sequoias, but, of course, they are much more slender in girth.

The Baobab (*Adansonia digitata*) holds the distinction of being the tree with the greatest girth. It measures as much as 100 feet round the base, but does not reach a height of more than about 60 feet. It grows in West Africa and belongs to the same family of plants as the Common Mallow which is often seen in hedgerows in England. A strong fibre can be obtained from the bark of the Baobab, and in order to get it the natives strip the bark from the huge trunks. This does not worry the Baobab, however, for even if the bark is completely removed from the lower part of the tree, it does not die but just grows a new layer of bark. The natives have been known to chop out the interior of a living tree and to make their home inside it.

The Banyan or Indian Fig (*Ficus indica*) is remarkable for the enormous area of ground that it can cover. As its branches spread out on all sides they send out hanging roots which descend to the earth and root there. The branches, supported by these hanging roots, can now grow much longer, and as they do so send out more supporting roots until the Banyan looks more like a small forest than a single tree. The great Banyan of

[*By Ewing Galloway, N.Y.*

Rafflesia Arnoldi, Sumatra. Said to be the largest flower in the world. When open it is three feet in diameter. When fully expanded, the thick, flesh-coloured petals are spread on the ground and a faint odour of carrion attracts numerous flies.

GIANTS

Nerbudda in India is about 2000 feet in circumference and has 320 columns formed by hanging roots, each of them as thick as the trunk of an elm, as well as numerous smaller roots. It is said that there is room for ten thousand people to shelter in the arcades formed by its hanging roots.

The common Groundsel (*Senecio vulgaris*), which often becomes such a weed in our gardens and is rarely more than a foot high, has a giant relative which grows high up on the mountains of East Africa. It is the giant Groundsel (*Senecio elgonesi*), which reaches a height of about twelve feet and with its large tuft of leaves at the top of the stem makes a very strange sight indeed. Another relative of one of our garden plants, the Lobelia, is also found in company with the huge Senecios. This is *Lobelia elgonensis*, which can be as tall as seventeen feet, rather putting our garden Lobelias in the shade.

[*Dorien Leigh.*

Climbing a Spotted Eucalyptus tree in Australia. Note the size of the man on the ladder. The maximum recorded size of one of these trees is 326 feet high and 25 feet 7 inches in girth at 6 feet from the ground.

The largest known flower in the world is the Great Flower of Sumatra (*Rafflesia Arnoldi*), which was discovered over a hundred years ago in the jungle of Sumatra by Dr. Arnold and Sir Stanford Raffles, after whom it was named. This gigantic flower, measuring three feet in diameter and weighing about fifteen pounds, springs directly from the root of the great forest tree-creepers. It has no roots or stem of its own, it is a parasite, obtaining all its nourishment from its host, the tree-creeper. When fully opened, the thick, flesh-coloured petals are spread on the ground and a faint odour of carrion attracts numerous flies. The life of this amazing flower is short; after remaining open for a day or two it begins rapidly to decay.

[By Ewing Galloway, N.Y.

A GIANT SEQUOIA WITH A MOTOR ROAD RUNNING THROUGH IT IN MARIPOSA GROVE, CALIFORNIA.

Many of these trees are over 250 feet high and well over a thousand years old; while the tallest is about 330 feet in height.

GIANTS

Although Rafflesia is the largest flower, another plant growing in the same region, the Giant Aroid of Sumatra (*Amorphophallus Titanum*) possesses the largest inflorescence. This consists of a mass of tiny flowers situated at the base of a column (spadix) surrounded by a cup-shaped sheath (spathe). The plant grows to a height of seventeen feet from a great bulb-like tuber, which can be up to six feet in circumference and produces a single leaf which is renewed every two years until the flowering stage is reached. In 1926 this Aroid flowered in Kew Gardens. It commenced to grow in May, and in August; when it had reached a height of five feet nine inches, the spathe opened, emitting a nauseating stench. Twenty-four hours after the opening of the spathe, the whole flower commenced to wither and collapsed a few days later.

The huge leaves of the Victoria regia Lily of South America are well-known to visitors to Kew Gardens. The plant is grown every year from seed, and sends up its leaf-buds to expand on the surface of the water into great tray-like leaves, six feet in diameter, surrounded by a rim five inches high. They are so strong that a small child can float on one and keep quite dry. The flowers, which are about a foot in diameter, are white when they first open, but gradually change to a beautiful dark pink, and after remaining open for a day, sink under the water to ripen their seeds.

The Sequoias are the greatest land plants, but even they are exceeded in height by the giant Seaweeds which were found by Shackleton's expedition to the southern seas: near Cape Horn these amazing Seaweeds were found to grow to 600 feet in length.

[*Will. F. Taylor.*

The great banyan tree, Calcutta, said to be the largest in the world. It is over 150 years old, has over 300 roots and is about 2,000 feet in circumference.

PORCUPINE FISH.

This fish is covered with long, sharp spines which can be erected and stuck out like those of a porcupine. At the same time the fish inflates itself to increase its size.

SOME VERY CURIOUS FISH

DRIFTING and basking lazily on the surface of warm seas is found a large fish well named the Sun Fish. It appears to have no tail, and looks like a huge wheel eight feet in diameter and weighing more than six or seven big men. Also in the tropics may be seen a peculiar Hammer-headed Shark, which is shaped somewhat like a hammer, the body being the handle. The eyes are placed at the two ends of the hammer head.

The quaint little Sea Horse has a horse-like head and swims with dignity in an upright position, but it spends much of its time attached by its monkey-like tail to seaweed. Little spines or flaps of skin looking like seaweed, grow from its body and make it very difficult to pick out in the tangle of weed.

The Trunk Fish is well protected inside its strong bony box made of specially thick, large scales, and from which only its head and tail stick out at either end. A hungry fish seeing a Puffer Fish and expecting a good meal is suddenly faced with an alarming problem, for as the would-be diner opens his mouth to bite, the Puffer

Photos]   *[Carthew & Kinnaird.*
SUN-FISH.

Note that the body appears to be cut short immediately behind the dorsal and anal fins, and that there seems to be no tail. This fish may grow to eight feet in diameter and may weigh more than seven men.

[*Paul Unger.*

SEA-HORSES.

These little creatures are unique in having a tail that can be curled up and a distinct neck and head that can be moved.   They swim with dignity in an upright position, but spend much of their time attached by their monkey-like tails to seaweed.

SOME VERY CURIOUS FISH

THE COFFER FISH.   [*Dorien Leigh.*

A peculiar denizen of tropical and sub-tropical seas. The body is literally boxed in with bony scales, the snout, the base of the fins and the end of the tail being the only soft parts.

swallows water and air and blows itself up like a balloon, and is no longer a possible meal.

The Porcupine Fish, a relative of the Puffer, not only can blow itself up but sticks its sharp spines out as does a porcupine. The Electric Eel makes electricity in its body and uses it to stun its prey. This monster, which may be six to eight feet long, can paralyse for awhile a horse or a man.

The Four-eyed Fish, which swims at the surface of a river, has each eye divided into two parts, the upper part for seeing above the water and the lower one for seeing beneath.

The Coffer Fish and the Unicorn Fish, too, are curious-looking creatures.

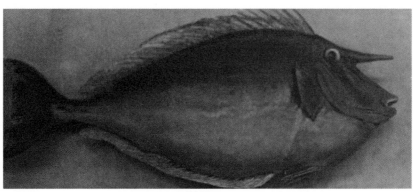

Mondiale]   THE UNICORN FISH.   [*W. S. Berridge.*

Note the long, bony horn projecting forward from between the eyes, whence the fish takes its name.

THE TRIGGER FISH.

When the dorsal fin (on the back) is erected, it is held firm by a knob on the basal part of the small spine behind it.

This fish comes from the Mediterranean.

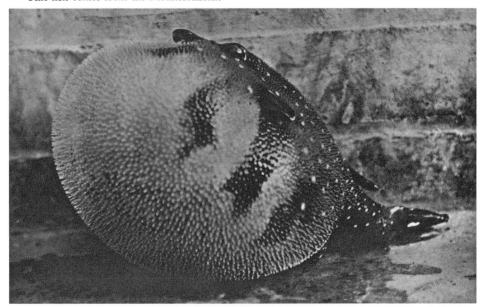

THE PUFFER FISH.

When annoyed or frightened this curious creature inflates itself into a round, ball-like shape and floats upside down.

CURIOUS FISH

COLOUR VERSUS SCENT

MOST plants depend on the help of insects in order to produce their seeds. The insects most familiar to us in this connection are the honey-bee and the butterflies and moths. Bees fly from flower to flower in search of pollen or honey and in doing so transfer pollen from one flower on to the receptive stigmas of other flowers. In this way fertilization is brought about and in return the bees obtain the honey and pollen they need for food. How do the bees and butterflies know where to look for their food? We think that it is the colours of the flowers which mainly attract the insects and the scents and odours lead them to more inconspicuous flowers. In support of this view we find that many of the highly-coloured flowers, such as many Gentians, the Cornflower (*Centaurea Cyanus*), Camellia, Pheasant's Eye

(*Adonis*) and the Lousewort (*Pedicularis*) have no scent but can be seen from a great distance because of their size and colour. Small and insignificant flowers, on the other hand, such as those of the Vine (*Vitis vinifera*), the Ivy (*Hedera Helix*), Mignonette (*Reseda odorata*) and Elæagnus give off a very strong odour which can be detected by the insect although the flower cannot be seen. It is probable that bees are attracted more by colour than by scent, for we find that the flowers which are specially adapted for pollination by bees usually have little or no scent. Flowers such as Salvia, Dead Nettle (*Lamium*), Figwort (*Scrophularia*) and also many members of the Bean family

(*Leguminosæ*) are often without scent.   On the other hand, the sweet-scented flowers such as Jasmine, Hyacinth, Honeysuckle, Pelargonium and various kinds of Catchfly are visited by butterflies and moths. One of the most remarkable examples of the relationship between insects and plants is the development of scent in some plants at a time which corresponds with the activity of certain insects.   The familiar Night-scented Stock (*Hesperis tristis*) gives off no scent during the day, but between 7 and 8 o'clock in the evening it begins to exhale a strong odour of Hyacinth.   Moths are beginning to show signs of life at about this time and soon they are attracted by the strong fragrance to the greenish-yellow, inconspicuous flowers of the Stock.   Other plants which give off their scents towards the evening are the Honeysuckle, the Pelargoniums, Catchflies, the Dames Violet (*Hesperis matronalis*), which has a scent of vanilla, the Tobacco plant, the Evening Primrose and many species of Petunia.   The flowers visited by bees, butterflies and other insects during the day often lose their scents when their visitors retire for the night.   The Grass of Parnassus (*Parnassia palustris*) smells of honey in the heat of the sun but towards evening its fragrance departs.   A garden Clover (*Trifolium resupinatum*), Spartium and Daphne also become scentless as evening falls.

A LIVING "FLOATING BRIDGE"

L OCUSTS are one of man's earliest insect enemies, and the destruction to vegetation and terror which they cause have often been described.   Yet it is only quite recently that the life histories of locusts have been more fully investigated and men are learning how to meet and check these plagues more successfully.   Migratory swarms do not occur in Britain, but in Southern Europe, Asia, Africa and America they arrive at intervals of several years.

Female locusts lay their eggs in batches of from fifty to one hundred in small capsules, which are buried in the ground.   On hatching the young locusts look very like their·parents except that they are much smaller and have no wings and so have to hop over the ground, helped by their powerful hind legs.   At this stage they are called "hoppers."   They start to feed on the plants round about them and are joined by other "hoppers," till eventually a very large band has collected.   Since there soon is too little food for all, they begin to move off in search of fresh feeding-grounds, forming a tremendous

Locusts that have massed themselves together to form a " floating bridge " over a river in Zululand.

Photos]   [*L.E.A.*

A " close-up " of a " floating bridge " of locusts crossing a river.   They are continually changing places with one another, some climbing out of the water and pushing others in, which take their places.

marching army, pushing and hurrying along. A strange thing about this moving army is that it advances practically in a straight line. Nothing stops the hoppers once they move off; ditches, hillocks, loose shifting sand, scrubby bushes and even rivers are conquered. The defeating of this last obstacle is perhaps their most amazing feat. The first-comers leap into the river and hold on to each other's legs and bodies. Those following walk over the backs of those already in the water and in turn fall in themselves, and hold on so that gradually a "floating bridge" of hoppers is formed, and most of the band can get across. To prevent drowning, the hoppers are continually changing places with one another, some climbing out of the water and pushing others in, which take their places. The majority get across safely, provided the river is not too wide and the current not too swift. When that occurs, the "bridge" gets swept away downstream. The floating mass of locusts may drift to the other side eventually, where they struggle out of the water, and are none the worse for their wetting. After drying their bodies in the sun they prepare to march on once more. The hoppers go through four or five moults and their wings gradually develop, becoming a little larger at each moult. After the last moult

Locusts tear and bite at the vegetation with their powerful jaws, scrambling over every tree, plant and blade of grass.

they become adult flying insects and soon large migratory swarms are formed, containing many millions of insects in each swarm. A swarm may suddenly appear as a tiny speck in the distance; gradually it gets larger and looks like a small black cloud. Nearer and nearer it comes; the hum of the insects' wings is heard; the light of the sun is hidden by the thick cloud of insects. They settle on the vegetation, tearing and biting at it with their powerful jaws and soon nothing is left but bare, barren ground.

[H. Bastin.

Awake.   Asleep.

THE INDIAN TELEGRAPH PLANT (*DESMODIUM GYRANS*).

In a strong light the small leaflets move up and down and from side to side. The movements are easily visible to the naked eye and last about two or three minutes, when there is a pause and the movements begin again. In darkness there is no movement, and the leaves assume a vertical position (asleep).

DO PLANTS "FEEL"?

THE leaves of most plants are capable of altering their positions slightly in order to present as large a surface as possible to the light or to avoid a very strong light by turning away from it. We notice that in a beechwood there are no, or very few, plants growing under the trees. The leaves of the beech are so placed to obtain the maximum of light, and do it so effectively that very little filters through for the benefit of plants growing underneath. When we grow a geranium in a pot and place it near a window, the leaf-stalks bend slightly so that the leaf blade faces the window and can obtain all the light available. This movement is brought about by the difference in strength of the light inside the room and of that near the window. A contrast to the beech tree, which casts such a dense shade, is the Eucalyptus tree of Australia, the leaves of which assume a vertical,

80

DO PLANTS " FEEL "?

instead of a horizontal, position as a protection against the injurious effect of intense sunlight. In this way the leaves expose only their edges to the direct rays of the mid-day sun, thus casting very little shadow. The Wild Lettuce (*Lactuca Scariola*) also shows this twisting of the leaves into a vertical position to avoid direct sunshine. It has earned the name of Compass Plant because it is found that the edges of the leaves always point north and south and the blades of the leaves face east and west, thus obtaining the benefit of the more feeble rays of the rising and setting sun. The Pilot Weed is another Compass Plant. It is found in the prairies of North America, and it is said that hunters have been able to guide themselves in these regions by means of this plant. When these Compass Plants are grown in damp or shady situations where there is no danger of injury from the direct rays of the sun, the leaf blades no longer twist into a vertical position, but remain parallel to the ground.

[*H. Bastin.*
The Wild Lettuce (*Lactuca Scariola*).
Left :   Plant seen from the east.
Right : Plant seen from the south.
This has earned the name of Compass Plant because the edges of the leaves always point north or south and the blades of the leaves face east and west.

The Indian Telegraph Plant (*Desmodium gyrans*) behaves very strangely when exposed to bright sunshine. It is a native of India, Ceylon and the East Indies, and has leaves consisting of two small lateral leaflets and a single large terminal leaflet. In a strong light the small leaflets move up and down and from side to side, while the large leaflets make the same movements to a lesser degree. See our two illustrations on page 89 ; 1, the plant awake ; 2, asleep. The movements are easily visible to the naked eye and last about two or three minutes, when there is a pause and the motion will begin again. In darkness there is no movement of the leaves and the terminal leaflet assumes a vertical position. No one knows definitely why the plant behaves in this way, but it is thought the movement takes place to avoid overheating of the leaves by strong sunshine.

There are many plants which are sensitive to touch, especially those belonging to the Pea family (*Leguminosæ*). The best known of these, which is often seen in hot houses in this country, is the Sensitive Plant (*Mimosa pudica*). At the slightest touch the leaflets begin to close up towards each other and the leaf-stalks droop. This drooping of the leaf-stalk is brought about by a very remarkable mechanism. At the base of the leaf-stalk where it joins the stem there is a cushion-like swelling

The sensitive *Mimosa pudica* in its ordinary state—

Photos]   [*B.N.A.*
—and immediately after being touched. At the slightest touch the leaflets begin to close up towards each other and the leaf-stalks droop.

(*pulvinus*), which consists of a hard centre surrounded by thin-walled cells filled with water. When the leaflets are touched, the effect is communicated to the pulvinus through strands of living material (*protoplasm*) passing through the leaves and leaf-stalk. The result of this message is that water from the cells on the lower part of the pulvinus passes to cells on the upper part, causing the former to become flabby and unable to support the weight of the stalk, which, therefore, begins to fall. After a time the water will pass to the lower cells again and the leaf will assume its original position.

BUTTERFLIES THAT VARY COLOURING TO SUIT THE SEASON

SEASONAL dimorphism, which means that butterflies can have two quite distinct colour forms at different seasons of the year, is a remarkable property possessed by most butterflies. Sometimes the two forms are so very unlike that famous zoologists in the past have been quite misled into thinking that they had found two distinct species of butterflies. The first Cabbage White Butterflies which appear in the spring have only small dark marks on their wings, but those which appear in mid-summer have much larger, blacker spots. This is not a very marked difference, but in some butterflies it is much more noticeable. These changes can be produced artificially and this shows that temperature plays an important part in determining which form will appear and that the temperature has most effect at the chrysalis stage.

Two Forms of the Same Tropical Butterfly.
Top : In the Dry Season.
Bottom : In the Wet Season.
The changes can be produced artificially and it has been shown that temperature plays an important part in determining which form will appear.

In the tropics it is not the temperature which varies throughout the year, but the dampness ; that is to say there are wet and dry seasons. The butterflies which emerge during the wet season are usually much darker and more strikingly coloured on both sides of the wings than are those which emerge during the dry season. The latter have coloured upper surfaces to the wings but the under surfaces look like dead leaves. Why should this be so ? In the wet season, life is abundant and there is not so much need for protective coloration, but in the dry season, when birds and insect-eating animals are hungrily searching for a meal, there is every advantage in being disguised to look like dead leaves when at rest. Probably the caterpillars' food, which would be green and juicy in the wet season, and dry and withered in the dry season, may influence the colour of the butterflies.

THE RHINOCEROS-BILLED HORNBILL.

This rare bird seals his mate in a hollow in a tree, where she lives in safety with her eggs and young, being fed by the male bird through a hole left for the purpose. He uses the big horn on the top of his head for a trowel when shutting her up.

SADDLE-BILLED STORK.

This is a large, black-and-white West African Stork allied to the American Jabiru. The bill is red with a black band down the middle. This bird frequents swampy ground and feeds chiefly on fish, frogs, small reptiles and insects.

SOME QUEER BIRDS

SHOE-BILLS OR WHALE-HEADED STORKS.

The Arabic name of this remarkable bird is *Abumarkub* (Father of a Shoe), because his beak looks like a shoe. These birds stand five feet high and inhabit the swamps of the south-west Soudan, southwards to Uganda and the Belgian Congo. Many ancient drawings showing Egyptian kings also feature this curious bird.

SOME QUEER BIRDS

THE GLORY OF THE CORONA.
The pearly-coloured upper atmosphere of the sun is only visible during a total eclipse.

HEAT THAT DEFIES IMAGINATION

A BIG blaze never fails to draw an excited, fascinated crowd. A forest or even a house on fire is always an impressive sight, but if we ask the simple question, " What is the Sun ? ", Science bids us think of *a whole world on fire—a world over a million times bigger than the Earth, and one that is burning more fiercely than the most fiery furnace that men can make.* We cannot do this, of course ; we cannot really picture anything like such a thing, but the very attempt to do so is sufficiently thrilling and awe-inspiring.

The gravity-grip in which this giant cosmic fire holds this little world of ours, also defies the imagination. Mathematicians solemnly assure us that were this grip, this mysterious, invisible force of gravitation, removed and some mechanical equivalent substituted, there would be required to keep the Earth circling in its orbit, a gigantic steel rod connecting Sun and Earth, *no less than 4,500 miles thick ; a steel rod actually thicker than the Atlantic is broad.* And this, mark you, assumes highest tensile modern steel capable of withstanding a snapping or stretching stress of fifty tons to the square inch.

Nowadays, we all know something of the importance of calories to the living human body. Newspapers, posters and doctors tell us a certain minimum number must be contained in our daily diet for A1 health and fitness. They do not generally make clear, though, what exactly a calorie is. Now calories are simply standard units

A BOLOMETER.
A super - sensitive electrical thermometer which records infinitely minute changes of temperature.

for measuring quantities of heat just as pounds, shillings and pence are standard units for measuring amounts of money. And, directly or ultimately, *all the calories that count come from our very old, very good friend King Sol.* Bloodheat is, in the last resort, maintained by sunheat. Organic life is a flame fed by solar calories. In a word, Science has shown the Earth to be " on the dole " of the Sun. What a lavish and truly magnificent " dole " it is too! On the average, well over one and a half million million (one and a half billion) calories shower down upon territories the size of England *during every minute of daylight.* What must be the sum total of calories radiated by the Sun, for the Earth's surface is approximately four thousand times bigger than England and for every single one received by the Earth, 2,000 *million go off elsewhere,* mostly out into the icy, inky, infinitude of celestial space? How big and bounteous is Nature! We cannot help feeling a little bigger and more bounteous ourselves when we think of her. Where should we all be without her calories, without sunshine? Well, the Earth would quickly become an ice-chest with the thermometer standing steady at 400 degrees below freezing (Fahrenheit). That is, showing 400 degrees of frost, *which is just about ten times colder than the North Pole is to-day.* The mean annual temperature at the North Pole is estimated at 40 degrees or so below freezing-point. Typical of the wonder instruments which have helped to make marvellous discoveries is the bolometer, a super-sensitive electrical thermometer invented by that noble pioneer of solar heat research, Professor S. P. Langley. The normal man or woman cannot usually feel temperature changes of less than 3 degrees Fahrenheit. The bolometer " feels " temperature changes *smaller than one-fiftieth of one-millionth part of a single Fahrenheit degree.* It can detect in ten seconds, a quantity of heat so minute that, *after falling uninterruptedly on a pound of ice for four hundred years,* the ice would still not be wholly melted. Such is the extreme delicacy and efficiency of the apparatus and tests necessary usefully to explore the secrets of the world we live in and to achieve the accuracy that is the very soul and essence of modern science.

HEAT THAT DEFIES IMAGINATION

Over three million square miles of frost and snow around the North Pole—a white waste forty times bigger than Britain—are melted every year by spring sunshine. Nearer the equator, great expanses of forest and prairie are set alight every summer by continued sun-scorching and are burnt to black, smouldering desolation. Now, every schoolboy knows how rapidly heat rays are weakened by distance. A fire a couple of hundred yards away would be pretty cold comfort to any of us on a frosty night, wouldn't it ! What then must be the original intensity of the Sun's rays when they are able to melt the polar ice and fire the tropic forest *after travelling over ninety million miles through a temperature hundreds of degrees colder than the bitterest Siberian winter?* (That is the Earth's distance from the Sun and that is the temperature of the boundless ocean of space through which its rays must travel to reach us.)

If we think that over, we shall find it not so hard to grasp Professor Langley's description of the Sun's aggregate output of heat. He said that if all the coal in the world's coalfields could be heaped together and a monster bonfire made of it, the heat so produced *would not equal what the Sun radiates in the tenth part of every single second.*

Wherever there is heat there is motion and commotion and noise. A kettle of boiling water sings and bubbles up and down. A pan of frying sausages splutters and sizzles. The kitchen fire crackles and quivers. Perhaps you will have noticed also that on a hot summer afternoon even the air is often wavy and tremulous ! Now the Sun's rays are about 45,000 times stronger at its surface than they are when they reach the Earth's. Is it any surprise then,

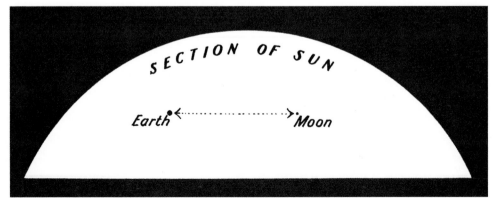

Sketch showing the size of the Sun compared with the distance between the Earth and the Moon. The Sun's diameter is over three and a half times the distance between the Earth and the Moon.

that the surpassing heat of the photosphere, the main radiating surface of the Sun, should be accompanied by noise indescribable and commotion on a corresponding scale? The Sun's surface is the stormiest sea known to man, and that wonderful instrument, the spectroscope, has enabled research workers to " see-in " or televise one of the most thrilling elemental dramas in all Nature. Gigantic explosions keep constantly hurling mighty streamers of fiery gas, called " red prominences," to enormous heights, *sometimes further from the Sun than the Moon is from the Earth*. Great tongues of scarlet hydrogen-flame have been known to leap up at the lightning-like velocity of 250 miles per second. A colossal flare-up has been seen to reach a height of 70,000 miles, 12,000 *times higher*

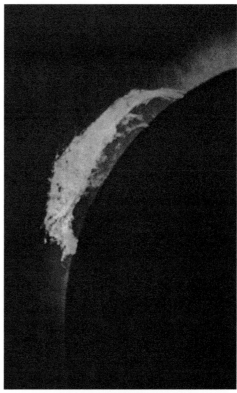

[By courtesy of The Royal Astronomical Society.
A SOLAR PROMINENCE.
Prominences sometimes rise farther from the Sun than the Moon is from the Earth.

than Mount Everest, collapse and fade from view in less than fifteen minutes, like some mammoth bursting rocket of the sky. The size of these super solar eruptions may perhaps best be imagined from Professor Simon Newcomb's (the eminent astronomer of the United States of America) statement that if placed in one, " the whole Earth would be as a grain of sand in the flame of a candle." The noise they must make can be imagined from Miss Mary Proctor's words, that, compared with them, the " crash of the thunderbolt and the roar of the hurricane multiplied a millionfold would be but a whisper." Mercifully, you see, we earth-dwellers are cut off from this demoniac din by a ninety million mile chasm of empty, airless space *through which sound waves cannot pass*. The lovely, flickering, coloured lights of the aurora are caused by streams of the minute, electrified particles shot out by solar eruptions, bombarding the Earth's upper atmosphere. Electrifying the atmosphere in conjunction with ultra-violet light, they also directly produce magnetic storms and the Appleton and Heaviside layers of ionised gases, *without which long-distance wireless communication would be impossible.* In exceptional force and numbers these little electric particles and ultra-violet rays from the Sun give rise to sudden radio fade-outs by excessively electrifying the air through which the radio waves must pass. Highly-electrified air, instead of transmitting radio waves, will extensively absorb them and so cause "interference," "atmospherics," and "fade-outs." Probably the first real proof of the close connection between fade-outs and sun explosions came to hand in 1936, when Dr. R. S. Richardson, a well-known American astronomer, found that a world-wide radio fade-out lasting a quarter of an hour, *followed within one minute of a big sun eruption* which he observed from the famous Mount Wilson observatory in California. A sensational proof of how these mighty storms on the Sun produce magnetic storms on the Earth occurred so far back as August 3rd, 1872. Professor C. A. Young, working with his spectroscope in the Rocky Mountains, registered three especially strong outbursts on the Sun at 8.45, 10.30, and 11.50 in the morning. Unknown to him till they compared

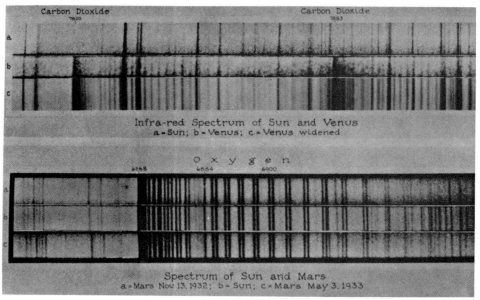

By courtesy of]   [*The Carnegie Institution of Washington.*

SPECTRA OF THE SUN, VENUS AND MARS.

The nature of the vertical lines and the position of each in relation to the other lines in the spectrum indicate the elements present in the planet whose spectrum has been taken.

HEAT THAT DEFIES IMAGINATION

DRAWING SHOWING THE SPIRAL NATURE OF THE SUN'S PROMINENCES.

Their rotatory nature is due to the fact that the erupted gases are cooled enormously at the vast heights to which they are thrown.

records at the end of the day, his colleague who was working on terrestrial magnetic observations, recorded three notable disturbances at exactly the same moments, one of which was violent enough to jump the magnetic needle right out of its socket. Inquiries later, moreover, disclosed that twitches and tremblings of the magnetic needle (indicating magnetic storms) had occurred at Greenwich Observatory *simultaneously with those of his own in the Rockies, 6,000 miles away.* The aurora is now known to be always attended by magnetic disturbances. Up to April, 1938, the greatest explosion ever known on the Sun took place in 1859. It was the only one that had ever been seen with the naked eye, the only one big enough to be descried without the aid of the spectroscope. Two exceptionally brilliant blotches were seen to break out near the edge of a sunspot and seventeen hours later a great magnetic storm swept the Earth and a most gorgeous aurora appeared, not only in the far north, but throughout Europe, the United States of America and Australia. According to the late Dr. G. E. Hale, an eminent authority on these things, this unparalleled cataclysm sent out a huge shower of electrified particles across to the Earth *at 90,000 miles a minute—a speed such as would take us from London to Cape Town in less than five seconds.*

In April, 1938, the greatest pillar of flame ever photographed was reported from Mount Wilson Observatory. It reached almost a million miles high.

The striking beauty and fantastic forms of the red prominences are no less impressive than their sheer immensity and staggering velocities. The late Dr. G. E. Hale, inventor of the spectroheliograph and one of the leading experts on solar research, said : " The best drawings are inert and lifeless when compared with the actual phenomena. These incandescent masses are vivified by internal forces which seem to endow them with life." " It is difficult to convey any conception of the brilliancy and fantastic beauty of the red prominences," said another observer. And Professor Young said : " Sometimes they are like pointed rays or hedgehog spines ; sometimes like sheaves of grain ; sometimes like whirling waterspouts ; sometimes like jets of liquid fire ; rising and falling in graceful parabolas. They frequently carry on their edges spirals like the volutes of an ionic column. All are spun of the same pure deep rosy light. It is unfortunate that no more appropriate and graphic name has yet been found for objects of such wondrous beauty and interest."

The great bulk of the materials blown up by sun explosions, of course, falls back upon the Sun and produces those raging whirlpools or revolving storms in the Sun's atmosphere called sunspots. Sunspots are in the nature of giant eddies or furious tornadoes five to fifty times the size of the Pacific Ocean and about a thousandfold deeper. Their rotatory nature is due to the fact that the erupted gases are cooled enormously at the vast heights to which they are thrown. They are, in fact, reduced to but half the temperature of the Sun's surface generally, and the meeting of hot and twice as hot gases leads to a whirling or rotatory motion. Nature always mixes opposing elements like these by this means, because it is the best

and quickest way to restore equilibrium or balance. To mix the milk and sugar with your tea you always stir them, don't you? The erupted gases begin to whirl round as soon as they begin to fall back among the hotter gases below. Their path down to the Sun again, thus becomes a spiral one—a corkscrew. Remarkable

THE AURORA BOREALIS, OR NORTHERN LIGHTS.

spiral whorls, almost like a spiral staircase, are plainly visible on special photographs of the Sun taken by a wonderful highly-specialized sun camera called a spectroheliograph. As mentioned on the previous page the first man to construct a spectroheliograph was the late Dr. G. E. Hale of Mount Wilson Observatory, and he has frequently seen on the Sun, clouds of glowing hydrogen as big as the Earth, trembling ominously on the edge of a sunspot and then finally sucked into the vortex *at a measured velocity of* 60 *miles a second*. To-day it is even possible to read the barometric pressure at three different levels or heights in the Sun's atmosphere, corresponding roughly to sea level, cloud level, and upper stratosphere.

How much fuel does Old Sol use? That is an old and bold question which thoughtful minds of many generations have asked. His fuel consumption must obviously be in keeping with his stupendous heat output, but the truth here is surely more marvellous and less conceivable than anything in the "Arabian Nights." *The Sun burns fuel at the rate of* 250 *million tons a minute*. Where can the Sun possibly get hold of such a tremendous quantity of fuel? Where does it all come from? Ever stranger does the truth become. He gets it from *himself*; it all comes from *his own substance or mass*. The Sun is ever and always burning up himself. He is shrinking and cooling —disappearing before our unsuspecting eyes at an unbelievable, appalling rate. *Ten minutes sunshine reduces the weight of the Sun by an amount equalling Vesuvius volcano*. The body of the Sun is being ceaselessly destroyed that his fires may be kept alight. Such is the sublime price of the life-giving rays which alone make the Earth habitable and fruitful.

How long can this flaming miracle of the heavens stand such a drain on his resources? How long is he likely to last? The answer, it seems, is: "Far longer than anything we can think of." The best and latest calculations indicate that over a thousand million years (a million milleniums) must pass before the temperature of the Earth controlled by the Sun drops by so much as a single Fahrenheit degree.

And no less an authority than Sir Arthur Eddington thinks that the Sun, which is simply the nearest star—our star—will probably continue to shine as a star of steadily waning splendour for 50 *or* 500 *billions of years to come*.

THE ISLAND OF THE MOON, LAKE TITICACA, SOUTH AMERICA.

THE LAKE ABOVE THE CLOUDS

IF we take our atlas we shall easily find in the centre of South America the state of Bolivia ; between that state and Peru, which is to the west of it, is the lake called Titicaca. It is the largest lake in South America, but it is not only for its size that it is famous. It is, indeed, more than 3000 square miles in area ; but it lies about 13,000 feet above sea-level. To show how high that is, we have to remember that 13,000 feet is the height of some of the great Alps, and if any of us were to climb the Jungfrau, in Switzerland, we should be only 13,658 feet above sea-level. But at that height in Europe we should be among the eternal snows, and it would not be very easy for us to stay there long. But in South America, on this lake so high above the sea, it is not only possible for people to live, but there are steam-boats moving upon its waters.

THE LAKE ABOVE THE CLOUDS

The natives who live by the lake have their own peculiarly constructed boats, which they make for themselves out of a reed called *balsa*. Our illustration on page 104 give some idea what these are like. We have to picture to ourselves this lake lying in a vast high table-land which the mountain ranges form in Peru and Bolivia. The city of La Paz, the capital of Bolivia, lies at a height of 12,700 feet. From that city a railway runs to the shore of the lake. That sounds very strange indeed when we think of what it means to climb the Alps or any high mountain and to be above the clouds at the same height.

[*Dorien Leigh.*

NATIVE BOATS ON LAKE TITICACA.
They are made out of a reed called *balsa*.

But Titicaca is in tropical country, and that makes all the difference.

From the railway on the Bolivian side the traveller can cross the lake and be in Peru on the other side. He will see on the lake the beautiful island of the Sun and the island of the Moon, which were sacred places in the eyes of the Indians who lived there. The latter is shown in our first illustration on page 103. He will see also many wild birds and flocks of flamingoes. The lake is still vast, but it is, they say, becoming smaller.

THE BALL-ROOM IN THE WONDERFUL SALT MINES OF WIELICKZA, NEAR
CRACOW IN POLAND.

A WHITE CITY UNDERGROUND

NOT far from the city of Cracow, in Poland, is a town which has
a name hard to spell and hard to pronounce : Wielickza.   It
is a place so unlike any town in the world that it deserves to be known.
Here, under the earth, in some places more than 1,000 feet down, there
are streets, railway stations, restaurants, shrines, and many statues
and monuments.   Here, too, are lifts and staircases, flashing with
dazzling light.   If we looked at the pictures, we might guess many
times before we hit upon the secret of this underground city.   That
secret is rock-salt.   In these mines out of which this city is carved
there is the largest supply of salt in the world.   Just as miners have
made tunnels beneath the earth to get our coal, so in this Polish mine
they have made this White City in order to get the salt which mankind

needs. But coal mines can never make a city in which men can live. The streets of this city run for many miles, and there are houses in it ; many workers have their homes in that city of salt.

When we think of the salt-cellar, it seems a very little thing ; and yet salt is one of the things without which human life could not be lived in health. Nor could man preserve his food if it were not for salt.

We do not forget the words of the Teacher who told His disciples that salt is good, and they were to be like salt in the world. But when we think of that salt-cellar on the table, and ask ourselves where the salt comes from, we must not forget that salt is in the sea and in the brine springs, but also in the mines of rock crystal below the earth ; and of these mines the most famous is this White City in Poland.

Let us spell it again : WIELICKZA.

[*Wide World Photos.*

A CHURCH IN THE SALT MINE AT WIELICKZA.
Here, in some places more than one thousand feet down, hewed out of the salt, are streets, railway stations, restaurants, shrines, and many statues and memorials ; also lifts and staircases.

TRICERATOPS.

In the age to which this three-horned creature belongs reptiles took the place which mammals and birds take to-day.

[*Mondiale.*

OLD INHABITANTS OF OUR HOME

IF we went to live in a very old house, we should think much about the people who lived there long ago. But we *do* live in a very old home ; this earth to which we belong has had many inhabitants before we arrived ; many relays of men, and of other creatures, for Man is not the oldest inhabitant by any means. We should like to learn more about those earlier dwellers in our home. Where can we discover what they were like ?

Before the oldest of records were kept by man there were the writings on the rocks, and in them wise men have learned what the earth was like in those ages before we came. These rocks are old sea-beds or lake-beds piled on one another. It must always be remembered that this earth has seen many changes :

> " There where the long street roars hath been
> The stillness of the central sea."

This is poetry and strictly true ; and it is also true that in the street down which we go to school there once roamed vast and strange creatures which no-one will ever see again. But from the rocks in which there are remains and traces of such animals, as well as from the fossils in which plants and animals can be recognised, we can learn what they were like, and in what kind of world they lived.

Here, then, are some of these old inhabitants. We may begin with those which are nearest to our age ; we say " nearest," but we must not think they were near to us as we count time. They are found, however, nearer the top of the rocks. When we pile a number of papers on top of each other and we afterwards go over them, the last comers will be the first with which we deal. So when the rocks are read the first creatures to be discovered will be those which are nearer to man than those buried farther down. So we may move backwards in the story of life. But we must not think of time as we do when we read our books of history. Here we deal with a thousand years as if it were a day. Nearer to us than some of the others was the sabre-toothed tiger. Readers who are learning geology may think of him as in the Pleistocene Age. He was larger than the tiger which we see in the Zoo. He was different in several ways, but what was most remarkable in him were the over-grown upper teeth, which were not so much meant for eating as for weapons. We have all learned the poem :

> " Tiger, tiger burning bright
> In the forests of the night,"

but terrible as the tiger must seem by night in the forests of India, he cannot be so terrible as this creature with its daggers in its mouth and its " forelimbs like grappling irons." In California they discovered the bones of many ancient creatures ; there was a pool there with tar on its edges, and many animals stuck fast in it ; among them a sabre-toothed tiger which had come after its prey and was caught ; and now, long ages afterwards, in that place we can tell the story of his last hunt.

Then there was the mammoth. It certainly wandered in what is " England's green and pleasant land." There was a time when the North Sea was a wide plain and the British Isles were part of Europe. The woolly rhinoceros and the mammoth roamed over these lands ; and the very early ancestors of man, who were wandering hunters, used to pursue these creatures. The tusks of the mammoth were larger than those of the elephant. He is best known from the remains which have been discovered in Siberia. This arctic mammoth was

" clothed in reddish-brown wool, and long black hair, while the tail was tipped by a large tassel of hair." These two creatures, the sabre-toothed tiger and the mammoth, we do not find it hard to picture, because we have seen their relatives, who remind us of them.

But we go deeper down into the past and come to the Age which is called the Age of the Reptiles, and now we are in a world which no human eye ever saw, with creatures unlike anything which the traveller can see to-day. There was the Triceratops, for example. He was a reptile. A " reptile " means a creeping thing ; but in the Age to which this three-horned creature belongs reptiles took the place which mammals and birds take to-day. It was their royal time. Reptiles then did not all of them creep as snakes do. Some had legs like pillars. Some ate flesh, but the Triceratops belonged to the vegetarian class. He had, as we can see, a bony frill round his neck, and on his head were large horns.

[*Mondiale.*

PAREIASAURUS.

These creatures were very closely related to the amphibia, and were not yet quite so well adapted to moving about on land as reptiles later became. Notice the very stout but short legs—not suitable for swift movements on land.

[*Mondiale.*

MACHAIRODUS—SABRE-TOOTHED TIGER.
This animal of the Pleistocene Age was larger than the tiger we see in the Zoo to-day. As the picture shows, he had over-grown upper teeth, which were not so much meant for eating as for weapons.

But further away from us still was the even more alarming Tyrannosaurus. He was not content to eat grass, but was a flesh eater. His teeth were like sabres ; his tail helped him to balance as he walked along swiftly on his hind legs. When we are told that his body was forty feet in length, we can understand how dreaded he must have been. This dinosaur, to give him his correct name, was not a vegetarian. Those who were like him, if they were to hold their own, needed to grow bigger and to move more swiftly, and to have teeth and forearms with which to kill their prey. But earlier even than this reptile—deeper down in the pile of remains—we find another creature, the Pareiasaurus. When we meet with him, we come nearer to the time when the first reptiles entered upon the great adventure of life on the land. They were very closely related to the creatures called Amphibia—we can think what this means by calling to mind the frog, which lives both on land and in the water. It was, we are told, a great step that the first reptiles took when they conquered the land. They *had* to do this ; the swamps were drying up ; the half-

and-half life of the amphibian became difficult ; it was an advantage to him if he could live on land. We see in the picture of the Pareiasaurus that so far the reptile was not quite so well fitted as he afterwards became to live on land. Look at his legs, very stout indeed, but not sufficiently so to make his movements swift.

Reptiles lived in the water and on the land, and stranger still, some of them learned to fly. We are told that five times the air has been conquered : by insects, flying reptiles, birds, bats and men. Man is the last to rise into the air, and he does it in a different way altogether. He does not grow wings, or provide a body which has a slim, light skeleton, and in other ways does not do as the birds do ; he has learned to use things which are not part of his body, just as he has learned to use a telescope for seeing, and a motor-car to carry him. But the Pterodactyl, a word which means "wing-finger," if he was to fly at all, had to be adapted in his wings and skeleton and bones. His size was enormous. The latest of these creatures of which we have any knowledge had wings with a total expanse of eighteen feet. When we compare the winged reptile with the others, it is interesting to note that it had no armour. It did not need armour as the others did. It is supposed that these reptiles began their new life in the air by doing

[*Mondiale.*

MAMMOTH.
The mammoth certainly—ages ago—roamed over England and parts of Europe. It had "reddish-brown wool and long, black hair, while the tail was tipped by a large tassel of hair." The huge tusks were, of course, an outstanding feature.

what the airmen do to-day when they use a parachute ; only the pterodactyl, or the creature who led the way, would have to provide in itself its own parachute. But if we think with pride that Man has made for himself a new world by learning to fly, we must not suppose that he was first. He was the last of the five.

By courtesy of]   [the New Zealand Government

A RECONSTRUCTED MOA WITH A MAORI WARRIOR STANDING BESIDE IT.

The Moa is an extinct, large, flightless bird of New Zealand. It was heavily built, some reaching a height of ten feet, or more. Eggs, bones, feathers and footprints have been found, and from these it has been possible to reconstruct the specimen shown in the picture.

The Book of the Rocks has much to tell us of this home of ours, this earth with its marvellous history. We ought not to forget the creatures that dwelt here long before man began his adventures. When we see the rhinoceros and the elephant still left, we shall be carried back into the past, when other creatures, long since dead and turned to stone, were wandering where our cities stand to-day. And just as we go back to the Ancient Empires, and try to see what life was like when the Chaldeans lived in Ur, so in the rocks we can go to ages far, far more distant from us, and try to see what this, our home, was like when those reptiles, which have long since perished, swam and walked and flew. They were creatures strange and terrible in our eyes, but they *were* old inhabitants of our home.

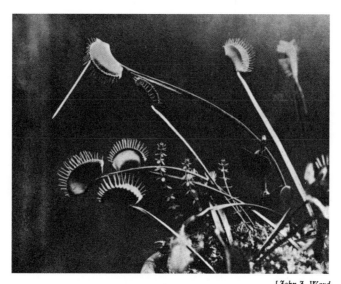

[John J. Ward.
VENUS'S FLY-TRAP.
One of the leaves is holding a pin, which it gripped on being
touched. The plant is a foreign relative of the British Sundew.

PLANTS THAT EAT ANIMALS

THE group of plants usually called Insectivorous or Carnivorous consist of plants which possess an apparatus for catching insects or other small animals and eventually digesting and absorbing them. These plants usually grow on peat-covered moorlands or in boggy places. In these soils there is usually a lack of nitrogen, which is essential for the proper growth of plants. The insectivorous plants make up for this deficiency by catching small animals, in the bodies of which nitrogen is present.

Probably the commonest and most familiar insectivorous plant is the Sundew (*Drosera*). It can be found, in the summer months, in almost any boggy place in the British Isles. The leaves of the Sundew are circular in shape and covered with tentacles, on the ends of which are rounded, knob-like glands. These glands secrete a sticky acid fluid. When an insect happens to alight on the leaf, it is held by the sticky glands and as it struggles to escape it touches other tentacles which curve over and hold the insect even more securely. The body of the insect is then gradually dissolved by the acid fluid and absorbed by the plant.

Another British insectivorous plant, the Bladderwort (*Utricularia*),

Flies creeping on and entering a *Nepenthes* "pitcher."

grows in stagnant pools. It has quite an ingenious and complicated means of capturing small water animals. Its leaves, which are divided into fine segments, are submerged under the water and some of the leaf-segments are modified to form tiny bladders about one-eighth of an inch long. The bladders are full of water and have an opening at one end, which is covered by a lid or valve which will open inwards but will not open outwards. If a small insect comes into contact with the bristles projecting from the lid, it is drawn inside by a kind of swallowing motion of the bladder. The lid then shuts and the animal is completely imprisoned. On the inner surface of the bladder are glands secreting a digestive substance, and as the proteins of the animal

are dissolved, they are absorbed through the surface of the bladder.

The Common Butterwort (*Pinguicula vulgaris*) is often seen in large numbers on damp hillsides in this country, especially in Yorkshire and parts of Scotland. In early summer its beautiful single blue flower on a long stalk makes it especially conspicuous. It is the pale greenish - yellow leaves arranged in a rosette flat on the ground which are responsible for catching insects. There are minute glands on the upper surface of the leaves which produce a sticky substance capable of holding small flies. When an insect lands

Photos]   *[Harold Bastin.*
Another kind of " pitcher " plant, *Darlingtonia californica.*

on the leaf, it is caught in the sticky fluid and also the margins of the leaf curve over and thus imprison the victim. The process of digestion then commences and the products are finally absorbed by the leaf. No insectivorous plant relies entirely on insects for its nutrition, and particularly in the case of the Butterwort, insects only form a very small part of its diet. Most of its food is manufactured in the green leaves by the normal process.

There are several carnivorous plants of tropical or subtropical regions which have very varied methods of trapping their

The Bladderwort (*Utricularia*) grows in stagnant pools. Its leaves are divided into fine segments, some of which are modified to form tiny bladders into which insects are drawn.

Photos]   *[Harold Bastin.*
The Butterwort (*Pinguicula vulgaris*). The surface of the leaves is sticky and covered with short glandular hairs.

insect prey. A well-known example is the Venus's Fly-trap (*Dionæa muscipula*), a common plant of the peat-bogs of North and South Carolina in the United States. The leaves are arranged in a rosette and are modified to form a kind of trap. Each half of the leaf-blade has a number of long stiff spikes on the margin and also three sensitive hairs on the centre of the lobe. An insect alighting on the leaf will probably touch one of the sensitive hairs. This causes an immediate reaction in the leaf; the two halves of the leaf-trap quickly close together, the two sets of spikes interlock and the insect is trapped. Digestive juices poured out by the glands on the inner surface of the leaf then do their work, and the parts of the insect which can be dissolved are absorbed by the plant. Charles Darwin, who first made an extensive study of this strange plant, gives, in his great work on insectivorous plants, some details of interesting experiments with it. In one experiment he made a small hole in one of the halves of the leaf after an insect had been caught. The digestive juice gradually trickled out of the hole and continued to do so for the amazing period of nine days.

Another group of insectivorous plants of warmer climates is that of the Pitcher Plants (*Nepenthes* and *Sarracenia*). These plants, with their leaves modified to form the curious pitcher-like structures, are found in tropical Asia, Madagascar, the United States and especially North Borneo. In *Nepenthes* the pitcher is the modified leaf-blade, while the leaf-stalk has become flattened and performs the function of a leaf. The pitcher has a lid which, although it does not close the mouth, probably prevents too much rain-water from entering. The rim of the mouth is very smooth and shiny, and honey is produced inside just below the rim. There is also a ring of downwardly-directed hairs round the inside of the pitcher, just below the mouth. At the bottom of the pitcher is a watery juice which is produced by glands on the inner surface. Insects are attracted by the bright red and yellow colours of the pitcher and by the honey inside. In attempting to get at the sweet substance, an insect will crawl up the pitcher, and, unable to obtain a hold on the smooth hard rim, will fall into the liquid at the bottom of the pitcher. If the insect manages to struggle out of the liquid, it is prevented from escaping out of the pitcher by the ring of hairs round the rim. When, finally, it falls back into the liquid, its body is acted upon by the digestive juices and is eventually absorbed.

[H. Bastin.

A house-fly caught and held by a leaf of the Great Sundew (*Drosera*). The body of the insect will be gradually dissolved by acid fluid secreted by the leaf, and absorbed by the plant.

CHANGE, CONTINUOUS CHANGE

THE evolutionist tells us that life began in the sea. From extremely minute single-celled life-forms, in the course of millions of years, higher and more complex types were gradually evolved.

Later on, when the waters had become crowded with living organisms, both plants and animals, many of them left the water to live first on the wet marshes, and then on the dry land. The descendants of these first land pioneers then continued to adapt themselves, and their anatomy, to their new environment, until they eventually evolved into the animals and plants with which we are familiar to-day.

Although the higher animals and plants may give no external indication of their lowly origin, yet there are sometimes links which show the path along which they have travelled. In the case of the amphibians—the newts, frogs, and toads—they present a kind of abbreviated evolution, and show us in their individual lives just how an animal can change from aquatic to land life.

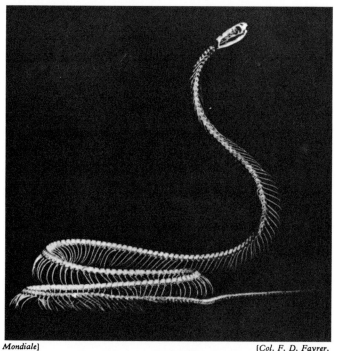

Mondiale]   *[Col. F. D. Fayrer.*

Skeleton of Russell's viper, India.

Their eggs are deposited in water amongst the water weeds, and hatch into little tadpoles, which are physiologically fish, for they breathe by means of gills. These gills develop to quite a complex stage during the first few weeks of life. Then the tadpoles' fish form begins to change, and limbs develop. Also, the gills shrink and are gradually absorbed. Meanwhile, lungs are developing, and for a short time the young amphibian spends a period in the shallow waters experimenting in breathing atmospheric air. Eventually its lungs become fully developed, and it then leaves the water to become an air-breathing animal.

Thus the amphibian briefly recapitulates its racial development from the single cell (the egg) in watery surroundings, through a gill-breathing fish stage, to a fully-developed lung-breathing land animal.

The reptiles—snakes and lizards—show an advanced evolution to that of the amphibians, for they have jumped the water stage, as it were, their eggs being laid on the dry land, and their young appear as miniatures of their parents—instead of as tadpoles.

All the higher animals, though, show in their anatomy traces of their evolution. The fish-like whale is really a mammal that has taken to the water, and its flippers are its fore-limbs modified for swimming. But all that remains of its hind pair of limbs are a few tiny bones embedded in its flesh.

Snakes, on the other hand, have lost all traces of their fore-limbs, but in the boas and pythons a few vestiges of hind limbs may still be found. Snakes probably evolved from lizards, and even some lizards have entirely lost their legs, as in the case of the slow-worm—which is, of course, a legless lizard.

In this way animals are continually changing and evolving new adaptations to fit them to their changed environments.

A Frilled Lizard.　　　　　　　　　*[Fox Photos.*

THE KING'S BARGE ON THE MENAM RIVER.

A CITY OF FLOATING HOUSES

THE kingdom of Siam lies between Burmah, which is in the British Empire, and Cambodia, which is French. If we look at our maps, we shall see that these three countries make up a large peninsula between India and China. Siam itself is an independent kingdom twice the size of the United Kingdom, but it has only one great city, Bangkok. To form a picture of it we must first think of the great river Menam, joined to which are a great number of canals. The city of Bangkok is built along the banks of this river and its canals and creeks. There the king of that country has his court. Some travellers have called it the Venice of the East, and it is certainly like it in having streams for streets and boats for buses.

The Siamese are famous for their floating houses, built on pontoons. Perhaps the nearest that we can get to such houses are the house-boats that we see sometimes on the Thames and other rivers, but these are mostly used for holidays and there are not very many of them, but in Bangkok they are seen everywhere. We can see, it is true, at any time, barges on our canals, carrying goods from place to place, but in this lovely Siamese city the rivers and canals are crowded as the High Street is in our city. But nothing that we can show is at all like the rich colours of the garments which the Siamese wear, and the colours of their buildings. Many of these are beautiful pagodas, carved with great skill. (Do you remember seeing a pagoda-shaped building in Kew Gardens ?) When the king goes in state down the river, as Queen Elizabeth and King Charles I used to go down the Thames, his royal barge is displayed in all its rich carving, and it has far more oarsmen than any boat which is to be seen on the Thames.

The Siamese are Buddhists, and to show their faith many centuries ago they built the famous temple Wat Chang. If we wished to reach it, we should need to travel twenty miles up the river. Then towering far above us we should see a vast pyramid with smaller towers by its side. It is indeed a temple, but within it there are many of the nation's treasures. It has, for example, wonderful art galleries ; and the devotion of the Siamese people for many centuries has enriched this Temple. It is certainly among the wonders of the East.

[E.N.A

LIFE ON A TYPICAL CANAL, BANGKOK.

MANY BRAINS AND NO BRAIN

THE nervous system consists of brain, spinal cord and nerves. In man and the higher animals, the brain is really the top of the spinal cord of the backbone which has enlarged to form a complex mass of millions of cells—a nerve centre.

These nerve-cells grow to great lengths, and their finer branches come into contact with the cells of sense-organs, as the eye, ear, skin, glands and muscles. In that way messages pass, by a kind of telephone system, to and from the brain, and so give us our knowledge.

In man, the brain is very large, and nearly fills the skull. Its average weight is about three pounds. Even the higher apes cannot approach that weight. The gorilla brain is less than twenty ounces.

Although the brain of the elephant is larger than that of any living or fossil animal, yet it is very small in proportion with the size of the animal, and is of low organisation.

The huge fossil Stegosaurus—a vegetarian Dinosaur—probably holds the record for brainlessness. The creature was about thirty feet in length, and its brain has been estimated to weigh two and a half ounces. Also, its spinal cord was enlarged near the middle of the back to form a much larger brain, to control the movements of its hind legs and tail.

This dividing up of the brain is usual in the backboneless forms of life. Insects and worms have a whole series of nerve-centres arranged in each ring of their bodies, each to control that particular area.

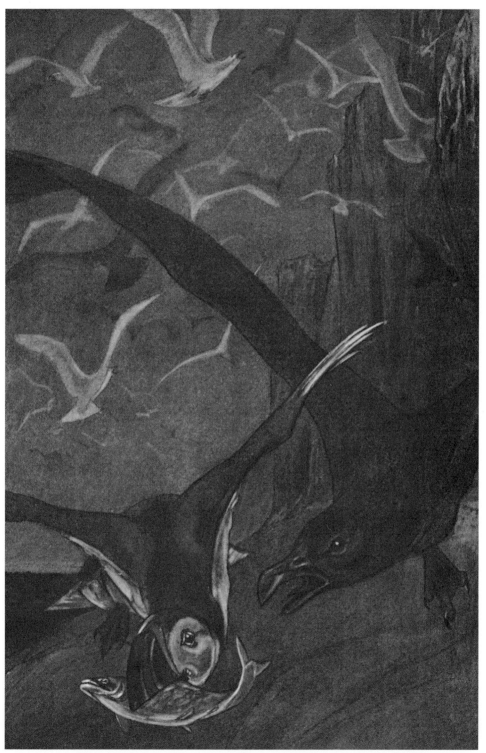

A SKUA ATTEMPTING TO ROB A PUFFIN OF ITS CATCH.

PUFFINS.

QUEER BIRDS

PUFFINS, or Sea-Parrots, as they are often called, live most of the year far out on the North Atlantic Ocean, but each spring many thousands come to the British coasts to nest in burrows either on small grassy islands or near the tops of cliffs. The mother Puffin lays only one egg, a white one marked with pale brown, and in about five weeks the chick hatches, covered with long, dark brown, downy hair. Its parents then dive for sand eels and small fish, and sometimes they come back to the burrow with as many as seven little fish laid across their beaks at once. The young Puffin quickly grows big and fat, but before it has learnt to fly or swim, its parents generally desert the nest, and leave it alone in the burrow to finish its development.

Shearwaters also come ashore to find holes for their nests, but they are very difficult to see, because instead of standing about in the sunshine outside their burrows, as Puffins like to do, showing off their beautiful white breast-feathers and gay-coloured beaks and feet, Shearwaters approach and leave their holes only under cover of darkness. One parent sits on the egg all day, and the other takes its turn at night. Most of their feathers are a dusky brown, and they have long, dark-brown beaks with a hook at the tip. Although they are so cautious when approaching their nests, once out at sea, Shearwaters fly very easily and beautifully, often just skimming the crests of waves, and diving into the troughs between them. They feed on shrimps, shellfish and other small sea creatures.

THE SENSE OF TASTE

THE human sense of taste lies in the tongue, the upper surface of which contains numerous projecting oval cells, known as " taste-buds." These cells are connected with nerves that convey to the brain our like, or dislike, of particular flavours. The cells on the tip of the tongue best appreciate sweet things, while those at the back recognise bitterness.

Not only mammals, but birds, reptiles, amphibians and lung-fishes are provided with taste cells in the lining of the mouth cavity. The lung-fishes, however, are really the exception in the case of fishes. Most fishes do not possess a sense of taste at all, and the tongue is sometimes altogether wanting. They mostly bolt their food with great rapidity ; although some species, like the catfish and the rockling, have sensitive whiskers (barbels) on their lips, which are perhaps associated with taste. More probably, though, they are organs of touch. The rockling also has a specialised series of ray-fins, which are kept in rapid motion when it is feeding.

Insects have most wonderful tongues, and we know that they possess a very selective sense of taste, but, in their case, it is associated with the sensory hairs of the tongue. On the tongue, or proboscis, of a blow-fly there are at least four kinds of hairs, each of which probably serves a different sensory function.

Mondiale]   *[H. Bastin.*

The immensely long tongue, or proboscis, of a Mexican Hawk-moth probing the corolla tube of the flower of a tobacco plant.

INSIDE THE CRATER OF VESUVIUS.
This volcano erupted and destroyed Pompeii in A.D. 79.

WHAT IS PUMICE-STONE ?

THE well-known domestic article, pumice-stone, is just frothy, aerated lava, often just the solidified " scum " or foam which forms on the top of a molten lava stream like the creamy " head " on a glass of stout or ginger-beer. It is very hard and is widely used for polishing and cleaning.

Steam is the chief cause of most volcanic explosions, and when a lot of it is present, it blows out some of the liquid lava into a light, porous mass, a sort of rocky " puff paste." The soft molten rock has been aerated just as bread has in a baker's oven. The moisture in the dough is turned into steam (water vapour) by the heat of the oven, and similarly, the moisture in the subterranean rocks has been converted into steam by the heat of the eruption, and it escapes as bubbles at the mouth of the crater. The holes in pumice and bread alike are made by escaping gas or steam—they are the cells or cavities previously occupied by gas or steam bubbles. Some pieces of pumice are so light and full of holes that they look like a petrified sponge. There is water in all rocks, as there is in all ready-for-the-oven dough. The fatal and

WHAT IS PUMICE-STONE ?

historic eruption of Vesuvius, which destroyed Pompeii in A.D. 79, turned many thousand acres of fertile country into wastes of barren pumice. Being so light, of course, pumice floats easily in water, and about forty years ago, the Japanese volcano Sakurajima erupted so much that for quite a while, *people were able actually to walk twenty-three miles out to sea on a vast "pontoon" of floating pumice.*

The mightiest volcanic explosion ever recorded, that of Krakatoa (near Java), in 1883, blew out so much pumice that the *Strait of Sunda was blocked to shipping for several months.* Some of it drifted nearly four thousand miles over the Indian Ocean before becoming finally waterlogged and sinking and getting washed up on the East African coast. Many metal polishes contain pumice that has been ground to powder.

The best quality pumice comes from the volcanic Lipari Islands off the Mediterranean coast of Italy. These islands include the famous volcano Stromboli.

[*W. J. Clarke.*

A FRINGE-TOED LIZARD.
As soon as a lizard is grasped, it casts off as many joints of its tail as necessary to enable it to escape.

NEW LIMBS FOR OLD

ALL spiders start their lives with eight legs, but usually these stick out such a long way all round their bodies that an enemy trying to catch a spider usually seizes it by a leg. The spider then exchanges its leg for its life, and escapes from the enemy with one leg missing. However, a new one soon starts growing underneath the stiff skin, but it does not show until the spider has "moulted." While the inside of a spider's body is

A GOLDEN SPIDER WITH ITS COCOON AND EGGS.

growing, the tough outer skin remains the same size, and when a young spider has been well fed, its skin soon becomes so tight, that it must be moulted and a new and bigger one grown. To do this, the spider hangs itself upside down from a thread of silk, and bends its legs together until it cracks the skin down its back. This soon shrivels away from its head and big body, but it has to heave each leg out of its tight, narrow tube of skin, and sometimes six hundred pulls are necessary!

The spider is quite exhausted at the end of its moult, and rests for a time, then carefully strokes itself all over before the new skin, which is soft and pale at first, has time to harden. When the old skin is cast, a new leg which has been growing underneath takes its place with the other legs, and the spider has its eight legs complete again. Sometimes the new leg has not grown enough before the

[*W. S. Berridge.*

A GLASS SNAKE.
This is not a snake but a lizard with no visible limbs. It gets its name " Glass " because its tail breaks off so very easily, and either cracks into fragments, or thrashes violently in the grasp of the enemy.

moult, and the spider then has one shorter than the others until the following moult. Most spiders cast their skins about eight or nine times.

Lizards also shed part of themselves in order to escape from the grasp of their enemies, but as their legs are short, it is generally by their long, fragile tails that other animals are able to catch them. As soon as a lizard is grasped, it casts off as many joints of its tail as necessary, and rushes into hiding under stones or heather or any other cover available, leaving the enemy with its tail. Often this goes on wriggling by itself, and so distracts attention from the lizard while it is escaping. Sometimes lizards even throw off their tails from fright, without waiting to be touched. For a time the lizard only has a stump instead of a tail, but this soon begins to grow and

By courtesy of] [*Carl Hagenbeck's Tierpark.*

A GILA MONSTER.
This is a brilliant scarlet and black lizard of the deserts of Arizona, in Mexico. It lives on smaller lizards that it paralyses and kills with poison which comes from its lower lip.

in a few weeks' time the lizard has a long tail again. In fact, lizards' tails grow so easily that sometimes if the old tail is just damaged, but not broken off, a new tail may grow out of the wound, so that lizards have been seen with two and even three tails !

Some lizards have no visible limbs, and although they are harmless, they look very much like snakes. One of these that lives in warm countries like North Africa, is called the Glass Snake, because its

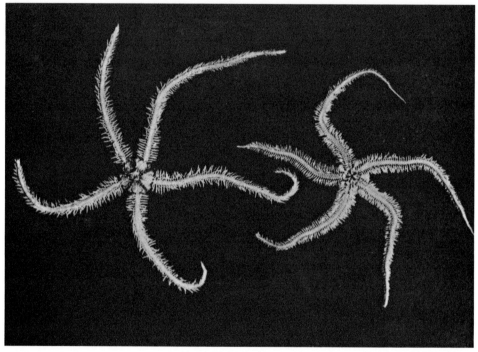

[*H. Bastin.*

BRITTLE STARS.
These very fragile starfish live round British coasts. They throw off *all* their arms as soon as they are disturbed, and so are difficult to find.

tail breaks off so very easily, and either cracks into fragments, or thrashes violently in the grasp of the enemy. The Glass Snake is one of the big lizards and sometimes grows to four feet long. Its chief food is rats and mice and birds' eggs.

Most lizards are timid and harmless creatures, which eat only spiders and insects, but there is a lizard in the deserts of Arizona in Mexico which lives on other smaller lizards, paralysing and killing them by poison which comes from its lower lip. This creature is called the Gila Monster, and it has a short, baggy tail instead of the

[*H. Bastin.*

SHORE CRAB GROWING A NEW CLAW.
Lobsters and crabs can regrow a leg or a claw if one is torn off in a fight. They do not, however, part with them on purpose to escape their enemies, as do spiders and Brittle Stars.

usual long, thin one. After a large meal, this tail becomes very fat and full, because the Gila Monster uses it to store reserve food in the form of fat, and it can live on this supply for a long time before making another kill. Other animals do not attack it because its poisonous bite makes it too dangerous, and it is easily recognised by its brilliant scarlet and black colouring. This is why it can safely use its tail to carry food reserves instead of to help it escape from enemies.

Starfishes can quickly grow new arms should they lose or injure any one of their five. Sometimes they lose and re-grow two or three arms at the same time, and in one kind which lives in the Red Sea and the Indian Ocean, each arm which is broken off grows into a whole new starfish ! This creature is called *Linkia,* and is so brilliantly coloured, blue and brown with black spots, that it looks like part of the coral reef on which it lives. While the new starfish is growing from a detached arm, it looks like a tiny comet, with the old arm for its tail, and these " comet forms " are so often found that *Linkia* probably sometimes breaks off its arms to increase the population of starfishes, without waiting for an accident !

We also have a very fragile starfish living round the British coasts, but as these " Brittle Stars " hide away in cracks or under stones, or in empty shells, and throw off all their arms as soon as they are disturbed, they are much less easy to find than the big solid " Spiny Crossfish " as the common starfish are called. They have long, fine arms and use them for rowing or lashing themselves through the sea, so it is fortunate that they grow very quickly, for even small noises or shaking make the Brittle Star cast them.

NEW LIMBS FOR OLD

Lobsters and crabs grow by shedding their shells and making new ones. Their shells are like suits of armour which cover them completely but are not living parts of their bodies. Therefore, these shells cannot grow, and quite soon they become too tight. A baby lobster grows its first hard shell when it is a little less than an inch long, but in about three weeks the inside of its body has grown so much that its shell is already too small. It then finds a safe crack or hole to hide itself, arches its back, and breaks its shell in a thin place just in front of its " tail " or abdomen. It then pulls itself out of the open shell and grows with a rush because in a few hours it must shut itself in a new shell—it cannot eat or walk or swim without one. The horny material for the new shell comes out of the lobster's skin, and very quickly hardens so that it can move about and eat again in a few hours' time. As lobsters grow bigger their growth slows down and they change their shells much less often. They are caught for food when they are about nine years old and have changed their shells about twenty-four times.

Lobsters and crabs can also re-grow a leg or a claw if one is torn off in a fight, but this does not happen so often, because their limbs break off only by accident. Lobsters do not part from them on purpose to escape their enemies as do spiders and Brittle Stars.

A STARFISH.
Starfish live on the sea-bottom and obtain their food by means of the numerous tube-feet that are found on the inside of the rays, or arms. By means of the tube-feet, also, they draw themselves over the sea-bed.

THE EXTRAORDINARY STRENGTH OF GROWING PLANTS

ONE of the most wonderful things in the plant kingdom is the ability of the roots and stems of plants, which are composed of the most delicate cells, to penetrate hard earth and to move heavy objects which obstruct their progress. The slender, thread-like roots of mosses and liverworts push their way into minute crevices in stones, breaking them up and dissolving substances that can be absorbed by the plant. That considerable pressure is exserted by the roots of growing plants, can be shown by growing bean seedlings in a layer of water floating on top of quicksilver. It will be found that the roots of the seedlings actually penetrate the surface of the quicksilver. The runners of several kinds of grasses (*Agropyron, Calamagrostis,* etc.) are covered with hard scales which help the pointed root to force its way through the soil. Runners of the Couch-grass (*Agropyron repens*) have often been known to bore their way through the roots of living trees and some have even pierced through the centre of potatoes. A paving stone twenty-one inches square and weighing eighty-three pounds, was mysteriously moved and raised an inch and a half out of its bed. It was found to have mushrooms growing underneath it, and these were responsible for the upheaval.

The penetration of snow by the flower-head of the little Alpine Soldanella is not caused by the strength of the plant. Very little force is required, because the Soldanella melts its way through the crust of snow. In the spring, beneath its white covering, the little plant is aroused from its winter sleep and begins to grow. The arched flower-stalk commences to elongate and as it grows it gives off heat, as most plants do, which causes the snow to melt round the flower-buds, where a little empty space is formed. Further growth can now take place and as the stalk elongates, the snow above is gradually melted away, until, finally, the flowers appear above the surface, where they open and look exactly as though they had just been stuck in the snow. Sometimes the flowers open before they reach the surface and one can see their blue colour through the thin covering of their icy home.

At times one sees walls of houses which have been cracked by the penetration and gradual thickening of the roots of trees. There is a well-known example of this root strength which can be mentioned here. In the Tyrolese mountains there is a larch which has rooted itself upon a large block of stone and its main root has grown down into the earth through a crack in the block. The gradual thickening of the root has caused the split to become wider and wider until one part of the rock has become completely lifted away from the other half. The root which was able to lift this mass of rock, weighing about half a ton, is just over a foot in diameter.

A toadstool pushing up a large stone.

[H. Bastin.

GIVING PLANTS ELECTRIC SHOCKS

THERE is always a small amount of electricity passing from the air to the earth through any conductors of electricity which happen to be in contact with the earth. This current passes through the bodies of human beings, animals, and even through the trees and plants growing in the earth.

The effects of very powerful electrical discharges on animals and plants is well known. Most of us know what a slight electric shock is like and we know that powerful shocks can cause death to animals and plants alike. When a tree is struck by lightning, that is, when a strong electrical discharge from the atmosphere passes through it to the ground, it is often killed or at least badly damaged. It has been thought, however, that a slight increase in the amount of the electricity passing through plants might make them grow faster, or in the case of crop plants such as wheat and oats make them give a higher yield of grain.

The first practical experiment in the electrification of plants was probably made by an Edinburgh man, Mr. Maimbray. It was recorded in the "History and Present State of Electricity," by Joseph Priestly, which was published in 1776. Mr. Maimbray treated myrtle trees with electricity "during the whole month of October, 1746, when they put forth small branches and blossomed sooner than other shrubs which had not been electrified."

The electrification of plants does not seem to have made much progress during the nineteenth century, but during the Great War the need for obtaining an increased yield of wheat, barley, oats and other crops from a fixed area of land led to the further investigation of this process. The chief method employed was that of an overhead electrical discharge. A network of wires was suspended over the growing crops, and through these wires an electric current of low power was passed. It was found that, with oats, the electrified plants became a deeper green and were larger than those not treated. Also, thirty per cent. more grain and fifty-eight per cent. more straw was obtained from the electrified crop. The use of this process has not, however, become very general, probably because, at present, the increase in the yield of electrified crops is not sufficient to justify the expense of installing the electrical apparatus.

About twenty years ago, experiments in the electrification of seeds were commenced and it was soon found that this treatment had as great an effect on the crops as the overhead discharge method. For this treatment the seeds were placed in large tanks containing a solution either of common salt (sodium chloride) or of calcium chloride. A weak current of electricity was then passed through the solution for a few hours, the length of time depending on the type of seed being treated. After drying, the seeds were sown. Wheat grains germinated earlier after treatment and there was an increase in the barley crop from electrified seeds of as much as fifty per cent. It is possible that more use will gradually be made of this process, because it takes quite a short time to treat a large number of seeds, and needs no very expensive apparatus.

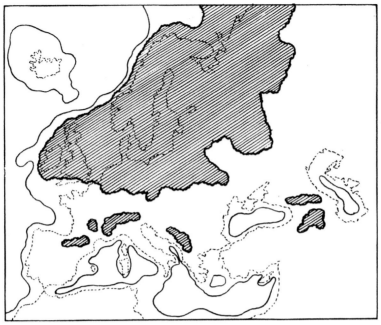

MAP INDICATING THE GREAT ICE AGE.
The dark part shows the Ice Cap.   The dotted line indicates the present-day coast line.

HEAT UNTHINKABLE AND COLD UNIMAGINABLE

HOW THE UNIVERSE IS RULED BY FLUCTUATIONS OF THE THERMOMETER

TEMPERATURE must surely be the least noticed of all Nature's ruling forces.   Without knowing (or rather realising) it, our whole lives and behaviour are, to a very surprising extent, a mirror of temperature readings.   Temperature is a Super-dictator, for see how completely and without fail do all things obey his iron laws !   Nothing can escape his decrees.   A mere thirty degrees Fahrenheit lie between the heat of summer and the cold of winter, for January is only 22° Fahrenheit colder than August, at least in England.   Eighty in the shade makes us puff and perspire and wipe our brows ; twenty makes us sneeze and shiver and wipe our noses (grown-ups at any rate). We all know that the living human body must be kept at an even temperature.   Indeed, so vitally important is this even temperature, that *a mere half-a-dozen degrees more or less than the normal of* 98°, *means danger to our health and sometimes even death.*   Though low down in the scale of life and intelligence, fishes are highly sensitive to temperature changes.   Dr. Bull, of the University of Durham,

Thermometer showing the mean surface temperature of the Earth at present, and also without the Sun, in degrees Fahrenheit. At Absolute Zero the last vestige of heat vanishes.

(Labels on thermometer: Earth at present — 60°; Temperature at North Pole — 10° Below F. zero; Earth without Sun — 370° Below F. zero; Absolute zero)

discovered recently that such common species as cod and whiting can detect in the water of their aquarium tanks, variations of *less than one-fifth* of a single degree Fahrenheit. Yet variations of *less than 3° Fahrenheit* can rarely be felt by men and women. The average boy or girl would fail to notice any difference between a room where the thermometer stood at 65° Fahrenheit and one where it stood at 68° Fahrenheit.

Not so long ago, geologically speaking, Britain was neither a green nor a pleasant land to live in. For hundreds of generations, 90 % of it was a big white waste of eternal frost and snow. We call that the Great Ice Age. How great a gulf between the frozen, uninhabited islands of that time and the fertile fields and teeming cities of Britain to-day ! Yet how small is the jump in temperature that has made this transformation possible ! *Experts agree that the mean yearly temperatures then and now differ by just 20° Fahrenheit at most, and quite possibly by just half that amount.*

Botanists find that such important higher plants as wheat, barley and forest trees do not flourish where the summer temperature is less than 50° Fahrenheit (the average summer temperature of Britain is 60° Fahrenheit). And, remember, where these cannot grow we cannot live, for, *directly or indirectly, the prime food of humans and animals alike is plants.* Temperature reigns over the world of dead matter as it does over the kingdom of the living. Strange to say, the condition of a substance, i.e. whether it exists as a solid, a liquid or a gas, depends very little on the substance and more than anything else on its temperature. Actual experiments prove that a sufficiently high temperature melts into liquid and then boils into vapour, the toughest, heaviest of metals, like tungsten, platinum and gold. On the other hand, a sufficiently low temperature turns into liquid and then freezes solid

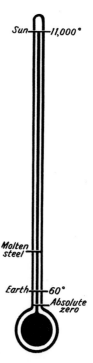

Thermometer showing the surface temperature of the Sun and the Earth in degrees Fahrenheit

(Labels on thermometer: Sun — 11,000°; Molten steel; Earth — 60°; Absolute zero)

the lightest gases such as hydrogen, helium and oxygen. At approximately 300° Fahrenheit below zero, the very air we breathe becomes liquid. In fact, liquid air is nowadays widely used for medical and industrial purposes. The range of temperature in Nature is immense beyond our ken. At one end of the scale, the bottom, there is the unimaginable cold of empty interstellar space, equivalent to roughly 490 degrees of frost (Fahrenheit). [In England, of course, we call 10° of frost a really cold spell.] At the other end, the top, comes the unthinkable heat of the sun and stars. The heat at the surface of most of the stars varies between 5000° and 50,000° Fahrenheit, while their interiors are hundreds of times hotter than this again. The sun is 11,000° Fahrenheit hot at its surface, while its central core is at the utterly inconceivable temperature of 80 million degrees Fahrenheit (80,000,000° Fahrenheit). See the diagrams, *Cutting the Sun in Halves* and *The Thermometer.* The highest temperature science can produce is 9,000° Fahrenheit. *Eighty million degrees is over 350,000 times hotter than boiling water.*

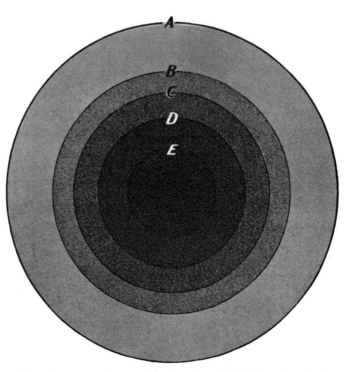

Diagram representing a section cut through the Sun, showing the temperatures at different depths.

A. The photosphere (outer radiating surface), 11,000 degrees F.

B. Circle 112,000 miles below the surface, 9 million degrees F.

C. Circle 175,000 miles below the surface, 18 million degrees F.

D. Circle 260,000 miles below the surface, 38 million degrees F.

E. Circle 330,000 miles below the surface, 63 million degrees F.

The innermost black ring is the central core, about 100,000 miles in diameter, which is about 80 million degrees Fahrenheit.

(*These temperatures are quoted by Professor C. G. Abbot from Sir Arthur Eddington's papers.*)

FULL SPEED AHEAD!

HOW THEY MOVE

ONE of the simplest forms of locomotion is that of the common slipper animalcule, a single-celled animal, or infusorian, found in stagnant water. It lashes its way through the water with fine cilia, which are much more minute than even the finest hairs.

A jelly-fish in the water is like a much thickened umbrella, with its mouth at the handle end. It is, however, devoid of any skeleton. Its jelly-like substance is controlled by muscular fibres which open and close the "umbrella," and that movement propels it through the water.

The garden snail glides along with its combined body and foot in close contact with the surface on which it moves. It invariably travels at the same pace (about thirteen feet per hour), no matter on what surface it is moving. Indeed, it always travels on the same surface—the slime track which it secretes. On that slime band, it can glide over even the blade of a sharp razor without injury.

A house-fly can climb up the smooth glass of a window with the same facility as it can up a wall. It can also walk in an upside down attitude on the ceiling. Its feet are specially adapted for such activities, each being provided with a pair of strong claws for the rough surfaces, and a pair of sticky pads for use on the smooth areas, such as glass.

The higher animals, of course, vary considerably in their forms of locomotion. A fish swims, and sometimes it may fly to some extent— as in flying fishes. Birds may fly, walk and swim. The limbs of many

animals become specialised for running, jumping, climbing, swimming and so on, but such specialisation always means some disqualification.

Man's limbs remain more or less unspecialised, yet he can, in a simple way, do most of the things that other animals do, but he excels all the other animals in having a specialised brain that guides him to use outside mechanical aid to attain his ends.

Faster than greyhounds are many animals of the wild—a buck pursued by a cheetah.

A large octopus extending a writhing tentacle upwards to capture an inquisitive turtle.

[*By Ewing Galloway, N.Y.*]

A MAN-EATING FISH.

The Piranha, found in the Amazon River, grows no longer than a couple of feet, but a school of them will attack and severely bite a man. They are attracted in hundreds by the least sign of blood, and with their powerful jaws will cut the flesh of the victim as cleanly as with scissors.

SOME FISH WITH MOST CURIOUS HABITS

ONE of the loveliest sights in the tropics is to see a shoal of Flying Fish leap clear of the water, their bodies bright and glistening in the light and their wing-like fins outspread as they skim swiftly over the waves. Sometimes, lifted by a gust of wind, they land on the decks of ships. It is not the " fin-wings " which give the power to the flight but the lashings of their muscular tails before they spring out of the water. Their " wings " then enable them to glide for as far as three hundred to four hundred yards.

Remora or Sucking Fish are capable of actively hunting for their own food, but reach fresh feeding-grounds without effort by attaching themselves by the suckers on their heads to powerful swimmers like sharks and whales, which tow them along. Occasionally they attach themselves to ships, and the sailors of olden days believed that these fish were able to hinder the progress of their sailing vessels, or even to stop them altogether. Lampreys and Hagfish attach themselves to

SOME FISH WITH CURIOUS HABITS

[Wide World Photos.

A TREE-CLIMBING FISH.

This unusual creature is a native of Borneo. It has no legs, but propels itself up tree branches by a combination of fin and scale movements.

other fish, but not in this case without injuring those fish which are towing them. They destroy their victims by rasping away the flesh, boring into their bodies and feeding on them.

We are in the habit of thinking that all fish must live in water, but there are a few which must breathe air as we do or would drown if kept under water for too long. For instance, there is the Mud-skipper of tropical mangrove swamps, which slithers about in the mud after its insect food, and is as agile as a lizard. The side fins are specially developed to assist the movements of the fish and resemble a pair of strong muscular "upper arms" with spiny fringe-like "hands." It is fond of basking on a stone in the sun with its tail dipping into a small pool of water. The fish's gills, like our lungs, can absorb oxygen only as long as they are moist, and while basking these might become too dry, and the fish would then suffocate. To prevent this, the tail is kept in a pool and by means of it the Mud-skipper is able to obtain the oxygen dissolved in the water. The Climbing Perch can breathe air also, and this enables it to remain out of water while it travels overland from one pond to another. This fish is peculiar in that it uses its sharp-spined gill-covers and side fins to help it to move on land.

In the tropical rivers and swamps of South America, Africa and Australia are found the interesting Lung-fishes, so called because their air-bladders have developed into lungs with which the fish can breathe air. The Australian Lung-fish spends all its life in water, but when the water becomes stagnant and dirty, as it is very liable to do during the long hot and dry season, the fish rises to the surface and gulps in air. During droughts in Africa and South America, when many rivers and lakes dry up for weeks or months at a time, the Lung-fish which live in these parts dig burrows eighteen inches deep into the mud and make

SOME FISH WITH CURIOUS HABITS

a protective case of slime mixed with mud round their bodies. The burrow is open to the air by a narrow tunnel. They live like this, breathing air and feeding on their fat, until the rains come and the rivers and ponds are filled with water again.

A little fish of the coral reefs called a Damsel Fish has the extraordinary habit, when attacked by an enemy, of seeking refuge in the stomach cavity of a huge sea anemone. The attacking fish in its headlong pursuit comes within range of the stinging arms or tentacles of the sea anemone and is killed and eaten by it. The Damsel Fish benefits by pieces which the sea anemone drops from its meal. We are uncertain how the Damsel Fish manages to avoid the same fate. It may be that the sea anemone does not attempt to kill the little fish, which seems to act as a sort of live bait for it, but it is more probable that the Damsel Fish is small and quick enough to avoid the groping tentacles of the anemone. A somewhat similar habit is that of the young of the Horse Mackerel, a fish found off our own coasts. In this case the protector is a large jelly-fish and when danger threatens, the young fish hurry under the umbrella-like body of the jelly-fish, and are protected by its long, dangling, stinging tentacles.

Several kinds of fish build nests, among them the common Stickleback of our ponds and streams. The nest takes about four days to make and is the work of the male alone. He produces sticky threads with which he binds weeds and sticks together to form a barrel-shaped nest open at either end. Then the male persuades one female after another to pass into the nest at one end, lay a few eggs, and leave by the other opening, until sufficient eggs have been laid. The male

[*Fox Photos.*

AN AFRICAN LUNG FISH.

During droughts many lakes and rivers dry up for weeks or months at a time. These fish then burrow eighteen inches into the mud, where they live until the rains come again.

now mounts jealous guard over the nest and fiercely fights off intruders until the fry are able to fend for themselves.

A nest of an unusual kind is made by the beautiful little Fighting Fish of Siam. The male blows bubbles on the surface of the water and coats them with a special saliva to make them stick together.

As the female lays her eggs, they are caught by the male in his mouth, carried upwards and stuck to the mass of foam, and then carefully guarded from all possible foes, including the mother who, strange to say, would not hesitate to devour them !

Most sea Catfish do not build nests, but the eggs are carried in the mouths of the males instead. On hatching, the young fry swim close to their father, bolting into his mouth on the least alarm. From the time he takes possession of the eggs until the young fish hatch, the father does not eat.

[*Sport & General.*

BITTERLING.

The female of this European freshwater fish has a long tube by means of which the eggs are laid in between the gills of mussels.

The Bitterlings make use of a foster-parent to protect their young till they hatch. The female Bitterling thrusts her eggs between the two shells of a pond mussel by means of her long egg-tube. The pond mussel makes use of the Bitterling in return, for as the Bitterling lays her eggs, the pond mussel larvæ are set free, many attaching themselves to the slimy body of the fish and remaining there until they are sufficiently developed to live by themselves, when they drop to the bottom of the pond.

The Archer Fish captures its food in a way which is not imitated by any other fish. It watches a fly hovering a few feet above the water or about to settle on a water plant, and squirts a small jet of water at the victim. If the aim is good, the fly's wings become entangled and it falls into the water, when it is gobbled up immediately.

[By *Ewing Galloway*, *N.Y*

DANGEROUS-LOOKING FISH.

Three sawfish caught off the coast of Florida. These creatures are quite distinct from swordfish. They often attain a length of twenty feet.

A BATTLE OF GIANTS.

A huge Orca Whale, "The Tiger of the Sea," has rushed up out of the depths to seize a giant Ray, peacefully sunning himself on the surface.

137

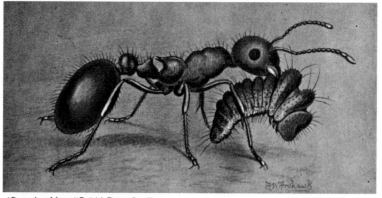

An ant carrying a young caterpillar of a Large Blue Butterfly to its nest, where it will feed it, care for it, and " milk " it.

A BUTTERFLY LARVA THAT HIBERNATES IN AN ANTS' NEST

OUR picture, drawn from life, shows an ant carrying off a larva of the Large Blue Butterfly. It has been proved beyond doubt that there is some strange affinity between these two creatures. Whenever a foraging ant finds a larva of this butterfly, it at once shows great interest. It caresses the larva and "milks" it, the larva giving off beads of honey-like liquid from a special gland in response to the stroking actions of the ant. Finally, when the ant has imbibed all the honey-like juice it can take, it picks up the larva and carries it off to the nest. Here it is cared for by the ant that first found it, being fed on ant larvæ until winter, when it settles down to hibernate deep down in the nest of the ants. In the spring the larva awakens and is again fed on ant larvæ until June, when it passes through its final transformation and emerges as the Large Blue Butterfly.

ROBBERS OF THE PLANT KINGDOM

SOME plants have entirely lost their green colouring matter, the chlorophyll, which enables them to manufacture food materials. They no longer need it, for they are the parasites, the thieves and robbers of the plant kingdom, living at the expense of some other plant and obtaining all necessary food materials from it. Most of these parasites have leaves which are very much reduced in size, because they have no chlorophyll and, therefore, cannot use the sun's rays to make food. The largest flower in the world, the Great Flower of Sumatra (*Rafflesia Arnoldi*), a photograph of which is shown in our article on " Giants," page 76, is a parasite, it has no stem or leaves: the plant just consists of this enormous flower which steals its food from the roots of a tree-creeper.

Probably the best-known parasitic plant is the Mistletoe (*Viscum*), which is usually found growing on the branches of poplars and apple trees. It was held to be sacred by the Druids of ancient Britain when found growing on the oak-tree. This plant is not wholly parasitic, however, for it has green leaves and can, therefore, manufacture a certain amount of its own food.

Other partial parasites among British plants are the Cow-wheats

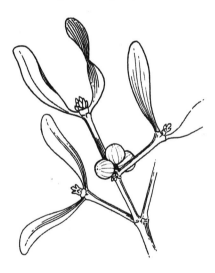

The Mistletoe (*Viscum album*) is parasitic on various trees, especially poplars and apple trees, and was held to be sacred by the Druids of ancient Britain.

(*Melampyrum*), Eyebright (*Euphrasia*), Red Rattle (*Pedicularis*) and Yellow Rattle (*Rhinanthus*). They all belong to the same family (Scrophulariaceæ), and they look very like other ordinary plants. They possess green leaves and are usually to be found growing in meadows where the soil is crowded with other plants to the roots of which they become attached. The parasites have roots of their own, but a great part of their nourishment is drawn from neighbouring plants.

The Toothwort (*Lathræa Squamaria*) and the Broomrapes (*Orobanche*) are complete parasites ; they are supported entirely by other plants. Even their seeds will not germinate unless they are in contact with the roots of other plants. The Toothwort is pale yellow in colour and is usually to be found growing under hazel trees, from the roots of which it obtains all its nourishment. The Broomrapes take their food from various plants. One kind is parasitic on peas and beans and another (*O. caryophyllacea*) on the Bedstraws. They are variously coloured, some being light brown, others are yellowish and many are tinted with purple.

[E.N.A

A male Ostrich hatching out eggs on the Veldt, South Africa. He sits for six or seven weeks on about thirty eggs laid by five or six hen birds, all in the same nest.

HOW STRANGE THIS SEEMS

SOME birds in Australia and New Guinea build little bowers or passages of sticks to use as playgrounds. They are called Bower Birds, and each kind constructs a different sort of playhouse, and chooses different decorations to make it attractive. One of them, the Satin Bower Bird, is a beautiful glossy, blue-black bird with pale blue eyes, and decorates his playhouse with all sorts of blue ornaments. He builds a little tunnel of upright sticks, and searches for blue feathers, flowers, little pieces of blue china or paper, or sometimes a few yellow leaves and flowers, and these are piled at each end of the passage. He then finds a female Satin Bower Bird to be his mate—she is a brownish-green colour instead of black—and the two spend nearly all day in the playhouse, chasing one another in and out, and arranging and rearranging the ornaments. Finally, they desert the bower and fly off to build a nest instead, in the branches of a tree.

Another of these birds is called the Gardener Bower Bird, because besides building a neat little domed house with two entrances, he lays down a " lawn " of bright green moss outside, and decorates this little garden with all the flowers, berries and beetles he can find.

HOW STRANGE THIS SEEMS

He keeps his garden beautifully fresh and neat, and always renews the flowers when they fade.

Many kinds of birds feed on insect grubs, and some have very curious ways of collecting their food supplies. Some African birds called Honey Guides prefer bee grubs to any other food, but as they are small birds like larks, they are not able to break open the bees' combs themselves. However, as soon as a Honey Guide sees a man, it gives shrill cries, and flutters about from branch to branch in front of him, and sometimes even flies in his face to attract his notice! Then, as soon as the man shows signs of following, the bird hops ahead and leads him to the bees' nest, and if he cuts out the honey comb, the Honey Guide can have its favourite meal of grubs. Another insect-eater is called the Oxpecker, because small flocks of these birds climb over the backs of African cattle and camels, and eat the ticks and fleas and fly larvæ which many cattle have in their skin. Woodpeckers eat grubs out of tree trunks and have strong beaks rather the shape of chisels for breaking through bark and wood. They also have very long worm-shaped tongues with a sticky tip, and with these they can pull a caterpillar from a deep hole in the tree.

Hornbills are big birds which live in the forests of Burma and the Malay Peninsula and in some parts of Africa. They grow huge, curved beaks, which often look like ivory, and in many cases the beak grows back into a great crest or helmet over the bird's head. This is probably useful as a hammer with which to break nuts. Their tails are long and their legs very short, so that they look clumsy and top-heavy, and when they fly, their wings make a loud noise like the puffing of an express train. Sometimes a Hornbill can be heard flying a mile away! They nest inside hollow trees, and as soon as the mother has laid her white eggs at the bottom of the trunk, her mate closes up the entrance with earth which he has mixed into a kind of hard cement in his beak. A narrow little slit is left, just wide enough for the imprisoned mother to push out the tip of her beak, and take her supply of food each day. She is shut inside the tree for many weeks, probably to protect her against snakes, monkeys, and other enemies, because she becomes very weak in the nesting season, and loses her wing and tail feathers, so she probably would not be able to fly in any case. Every day the father bird brings her a little white bag, about the size of a hen's egg, filled with bits of leaf and fruit for her food. This bag is the inner lining of his gizzard, which he throws off full of food, and grows again each day. It is not surprising that he becomes very thin as a result of this arrangement and sometimes even dies of exhaustion! Then other Hornbills come and feed the mother through the slit. Finally, when the young birds have grown feathers and are ready to leave the nest, the father and mother together break the block which made her a prisoner, and the family is free to fly away.

The Weaver Birds of South Africa like nesting in company, and sometimes a hundred or more pairs nest in a single palm tree. The nests

A snake having lowered itself in an attempt to rob a Weaver Bird's nest, is attacked by the infuriated occupants.

are made of fine strips of palm leaf and grass, woven into the shape of a little bag or water bottle (as shown in our illustration), and to protect the eggs and young birds from snakes, they are hung as far out of reach as possible. Sociable Weaver Birds first pile a mass of sticks and grass big enough to fill a farm cart, on the branches of camel-thorn trees. The piles are generally the shape of umbrellas or haycocks, and flat underneath. In this flat under-surface, many pairs of Sociable Weaver Birds make holes, both to hide their nests and to shelter themselves against rain and wind.

Ostriches have to make their nests on the ground as these birds are too big to sit in bushes or trees, and just before the nesting season, flocks of ostriches split up into little family parties made up of one father ostrich and five or six mothers, and each little party finds as wild a place as possible for nesting. The father has to make the nest ; he scrapes out a shallow hole in the sand and all the mothers lay their eggs in this. They lay about thirty eggs between them, but they do very little else for their families. They leave all the incubating to the father, who sits faithfully every night for six or seven weeks, though during the day he often hides the eggs with sand and goes away from the nest, leaving them to be kept warm by the strong sun.

Motmots are birds that live in thick forests in South America, and spend much of their time perching on the branch of a tree, swaying their long, strange-shaped tail feathers, then darting off suddenly in pursuit of insects. Young Motmots, when their tail feathers are growing after the first moult, are kept busy stripping little bits off the middle pair with their beaks, until they make the tips of these feathers look like two tiny tennis rackets on the end of long, thin handles.

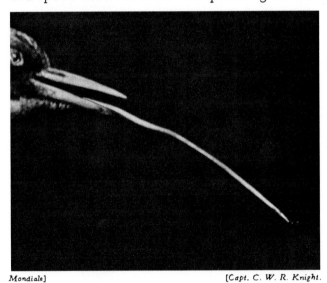

Mondiale]   *[Capt. C. W. R. Knight.*

The long and worm-shaped tongue of a Green Woodpecker. With it the bird can pull a caterpillar or ants and their eggs from a deep hole in a tree.

MANY, MANY MILLIONS

MANY of the flowering plants produce very large numbers of seeds every year. Annual plants such as the Flixweed (*Sisymbrium Sophia*) and Shepherd's Purse (*Capsella Bursa-pastoris*) give rise to enormous numbers of seeds, of which thousands are wasted. The former has been estimated to produce about 730,000 and the latter 64,000 seeds. As the populations of these plants do not increase to any great extent, it seems that about 10,000 seeds are wasted for every one that germinates and becomes a fully-grown plant. The Tobacco Plant (*Nicotiana Tabacum*) yields about 360,000, the Wild Radish (*Raphanus Raphanistrum*), 12,000, the Great Plantain (*Plantago major*), 14,000, and the Henbane (*Hyoscyamus niger*), 10,000 seeds. If all the 730,000 seeds of a Flixweed plant were to germinate and produce plants each of which again produced 730,000 seeds, and this multiplication were to go on for three years, an area two thousand times as great as the whole of the dry land in the world would be covered with the plants. Fortunately, large numbers of the seeds never reach ground suitable for germination, others are devoured by birds and insects, and the sea separating one country from another is an effective barrier against unrestricted distribution.

The largest numbers of seeds are produced by the Orchidaceæ. In this Family the seeds are often very small indeed, almost dust-like, and they can easily be blown about and carried by the wind. The record for the highest number of seeds produced by one plant is probably held by an Orchid from Gùiana called *Cycnoches chlorochilon*. It was estimated that there were the almost unbelievable number of 3,770,000 seeds in one capsule ! The seeds were not actually counted but the approximate number was obtained by weighing a known number of seeds, dividing this weight into the total weight of all the seeds and then a simple calculation gave the total number of seeds in the capsule. Another Orchid (*Maxillaria*), which is found in Brazil, is said to have one and three quarter millions of seeds in one capsule and as it produces about six capsules in one season, the total number of seeds must be in the region of ten millions.

Ferns produce large numbers of spores in one year, but they are so small that an attempt to make any estimate of their number would be futile. One gets some idea of this by walking through bracken in the late summer or autumn. The spores rise up in rusty brown clouds and one's clothes soon become quite brown with them. Other plants which produce spores in large numbers are those belonging to the Fungus group. Their spores are so light that they float about freely in the air and they are so small that we cannot easily see them. We can prove that there are spores present in a room by leaving a piece of bread exposed to the air and keeping it quite damp. In a few days the bread will be covered with a greenish-blue mould which has grown from spores present in the atmosphere.

We find, as might be expected, that the larger seeds are not produced in very great numbers. The Cocoa-nut Palm does not bear more than a few hundred nuts in one season. These nuts usually weigh about two pounds, but those of the Seychelles Palm (*Lodoicea Sechellarum*) are about ten pounds in weight and often as much as a foot in length. The largest fruits, however, are those of the Gourds and Pumpkins. The Melon-pumpkin (*Cucurbita maxima*) has a fruit with a diameter of over three feet, which weighs about two hundred pounds, and the Bottle-gourd (*Lagenaria*) has been known to produce fruit over four feet long and about one foot in diameter.

There is great variation in the length of time that seeds will remain dormant. By dormancy we mean that the seeds are " resting "; they are alive but they will not germinate because conditions are not suitable. Some seeds will not germinate under any conditions until some time has elapsed after their dispersal, while others, such as those of the Willows and Poplars, do not retain their power of germination for more than a day or two.

Most garden seeds will not remain alive for more than a year or so, but many members of the Pea Family (*Leguminosæ*) have very long-lived seeds. The seed of a Trifolium (*Trifolium striatum*) has germinated after ninety years, a Cytisus after eighty-seven years and Lentil seeds (*Lens esculenta*) after sixty-five years. The longest recorded period for which seeds have retained their vitality is about one hundred and fifty years. The seeds were those of a Water Lily (*Nelumbo*) and they were taken from collections in the British Museum and sown by Robert Brown, the famous botanist, in 1850. He succeeded in germinating about eighty per cent. of the seeds.

The seeds of weeds can lie dormant beneath the soil for long periods. When old pastures are ploughed up, numerous weeds such as Charlock and Trefoil spring up from the dormant seed which has been brought to the surface, where it is able to germinate.

By courtesy of]   [The Imperial Institute of Entomology.

Coco-nut palm-trees recovering after an insect parasite had been established to combat a plague of destructive moths. The young new leaves are all entirely green, the old or lower ones, white or grey.

"SET A THIEF——"

WHEN insects become very numerous and start to eat up our crops and spoil our fruit, we call them pests, for example, caterpillars of the Cabbage White Butterfly, green-flies and fruit-flies. Sometimes we can control insect pests by spraying chemicals on to them and their food plants, but this is not always successful, and they may continue to increase in numbers and do damage in spite of our efforts to check them. So man has discovered another way of stopping the destruction, and that is to get some other living creature to kill off the pests for us.

This method of fighting insect pests is called biological control. It is not always an easy matter to find just the right sort of living creature which will do it satisfactorily. Sometimes the one employed, particularly if it has been brought into a new country from its natural home in some foreign land, gets out of control itself when let loose, and it may multiply rapidly and sometimes become a worse pest than the insect which people hoped would be killed off by its efforts. This has happened several times in the past and so scientists have to be exceedingly careful. Therefore, the creature which is going to be used to help us control the pest must be imprisoned and watched carefully for some time before it is set free, in case it should change its way of living when in the new country.

Little Owls were not found in this country fifty years ago. Someone thought it would be a good idea to bring some Little Owls to England from Holland and let them catch our field mice, which became so numerous from time to time as to become pests. The Little Owls soon increased in numbers and did kill many mice, but they found it easy to kill some of our useful birds as well, like thrushes, blackbirds and finches. That was one mistake Man made. Here is another. Mongooses were taken to the West Indies to kill off rats which attacked and spoilt large quantities of sugar cane. They quickly killed off most of the rats, and the owners of the sugar cane plantations were congratulating themselves on all the money they would now save. The mongooses, however, finding after a while that rats were scarce, began to feed on birds, birds' eggs, poultry, kids and calves, fruit and even sugar cane, which was, perhaps, the biggest insult of all, since they had been brought to Jamaica especially to guard it. So in the end they became much more serious pests than the rats.

Why should this be so ? Usually an animal in its native or home country does not behave like this, because either its many enemies or its various diseases keep it from multiplying and becoming a plague. In a new country there are too few natural enemies, and

A LITTLE OWL.
Fifty years ago Little Owls were not found in Great Britain. They were introduced, however, to catch field mice. Now they kill many of our useful birds as well.

so it gets out of control, or as we might
say, the balance of nature is upset.

Here are some examples of the
successful control of insect pests by
biological methods.   Fortunately, in
Britain we do not suffer badly from
insect pests, but in America,
Africa, Australia and New
Zealand, serious outbreaks
occur.   In nearly all cases
the pests (frequently insects)
have been introduced from
other   countries,   usually
accidentally,   of   course,
many having been trans-
ported along with cargo.
T h e y   s t a r t   t o   d o
tremendous   damage   in
their new homes, because
their natural enemies, like
birds, small mammals, and
other   insects,   have   been
left behind, and so there

A MONGOOSE.
Mongooses were taken to the West Indies to destroy
rats. Having killed off most of the rats they began to
feed on birds, poultry, kids and calves, and fruit, and
became much more serious pests than the rats.

is nothing to stop them from spreading.   The first really startling
and successful experiment in pest control happened in 1886.   About
1870 some small orange trees were shipped to California from Australia
and replanted.   Nobody noticed at first the few tiny little scales
which appeared on the fruit, but in ten years' time they had grown
slightly larger and far more numerous and had spread through all
the orange and lemon groves.   These were found to be scale insects
called Cottony Cushion Scales.   The female Cottony Cushion Scales
cannot fly and they secrete quantities of fluffy wax which sticks to
their cast skins and forms a kind of scale beneath which they live
and bring up their young, not moving at all, since the scale becomes
stuck fast to the fruit.   Scale insects are very serious pests because
they feed on the juices of fruit trees, spoiling the fruit and the trees
too, and doing a tremendous amount of damage.   Chemical sprays
were found to be of no use against the orange and lemon scales.
However, scientists were able to get rid of this pest by finding one

of its natural enemies, a ladybird in Australia, which is extraordinarily good at killing the scales, seeking them out most greedily. About one dozen ladybirds in the resting stage were posted to California. Many were reared from these and were put on an orange tree badly attacked by scale insects. The tree was covered with a tent and watched closely. When the scientists were satisfied that it would be safe to let the ladybirds escape and start to work on the avenues of fruit trees, the tent was removed and they were then free. The ladybird beetles themselves had none of their own particular enemies in California and so rapidly grew in numbers, and in less than five years the troublesome scale insects were practically exterminated.

Since this was so successful an experiment, the same kind of ladybird beetles have been taken to South Africa, New Zealand, Japan, Egypt, Florida, Hawaii, Portugal, Italy, South of France and Malta, and have successfully killed off pests of scale insects in these countries.

Similarly, the Woolly Aphis pest, which attacks apple trees, is found all over the world. The adult and young secrete, near the hind end of the body, a fluffy wax with a " woolly " appearance. This " wool " helps to protect them. They feed on the young shoots of trees and their puncture marks allow the sap to escape, and disease germs can enter and damage the tree. Cankers or rough swellings form due to the irritation. An enemy has been found, another insect, which lays its eggs inside the larvæ of the aphis. The enemy larvæ eat up the aphis larvæ from inside gradually, crawling out of the old dead skin afterwards. This enemy was found in North America and has been introduced with excellent results into New Zealand, South America, Italy, and Australia, and with fairly good results into South Africa, Germany and Holland.

In Fiji, the coco-nut palm is a very important tree, since it is a source of food, fibre and especially copra, which forms a most valuable trade. Copra is the dried, broken-up white flesh of the coco-nut, from which coco-nut oil is obtained. About fifty years ago many of the trees in Fiji began to lose their leaves, until in some plantations only bare trunks were left. A kind of moth was found to be the cause of the damage. The caterpillars of this moth devoured the leaves, and the coco-nut crop began to fail. The pest spread from one island to another, till things looked desperate. Rewards were offered for a cure for the pest. In Malaya, an enemy was eventually found for the moth, a kind of fly. Eventually about three hundred of these flies were brought over in 1925, and in three years' time, the plague of coco-nut moth caterpillars was checked. This was a very rapid cure, and the coco-nut industry in Fiji is now safe.

Weeds can also be pests, since they choke out more useful plants and may turn areas of the country into waste land. As with insect pests, it is generally those plants which have been introduced from other countries which start to run wild, and cannot be kept under control by farming operations or chemical sprays. Insects have been employed to help us to kill the weeds, and sometimes this has been very successful. Care must be taken, though, to make sure that the insects to be used do feed in their own countries only on the particular weed plant we wish to stamp out, before we risk taking them to another land. It would be disastrous if they wandered off the weed plants and started taking a fancy to other plants like our crops, for instance. There is a troublesome weed in Australia called the Prickly Pear. It is not a pear, but a kind of spiny cactus, which was taken to Australia from America and was at first a garden plant. But it soon escaped from the gardens and spread

The Prickly Pear Cactus was taken from America to Australia, where it quickly spread and became a pest. Eventually insects were found that would feed on the Prickly Pear and keep it under control.

far and wide, until in 1925 it covered sixty million acres of land and each year spread over another million acres. In its home in America, insects and plant diseases kept it within bounds, but in Australia there were no such insects or diseases to stop its growth. At last, after searching laboriously in America and the West Indies for enemies of the Prickly Pear, four chief ones were found. These were carefully tested out and allowed to become accustomed to Australian weather, before being set free. The enemies eat the Prickly Pear with such enjoyment that they never touch any other food and starve to death if there are no Prickly Pear plants near. By 1929 these four enemies had done a great deal of good. In 1930, numbers of another enemy, a moth, were set free and in five years' time, the pest was checked, and acres of land cleared from these unpleasant prickly bushes. The larvæ of this moth bore into the plants, feeding on the juicy stems. Disease germs attack the plants, entering through the holes the larvæ have made, till eventually the Prickly Pears become rotting masses of pulp. In all the examples of successful control

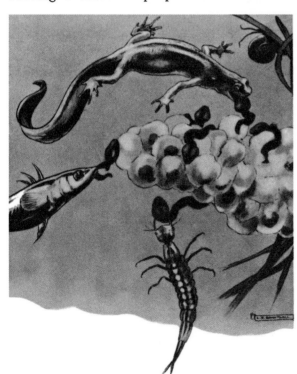

which you have just read about, invertebrate animals were used; that is, creatures without a backbone. Man does occasionally employ vertebrate animals like fish, birds and mammals, but on the whole they are more liable to alter their habits in a new country than invertebrates are, and so are somewhat dangerous. Fish have been used very successfully to feed on the larvæ of mosquitoes, which carry malaria and yellow fever, two dread diseases of Man. By this means the numbers of mosquitoes have been reduced, and the diseases prevented from spreading.

Tadpoles are no sooner hatched than numerous enemies assemble to devour them.

LIVES LONG AND SHORT

GREAT bodily size in animals does not necessarily indicate a long life. The elephant lives but little longer than Man. It is getting old at 70, but may live to be over 100, but 150 years is unlikely. Hippopotami and rhinoceroses come next with a somewhat lower average, and probably never reach 100 years.

The horse has been known to attain 53 years, and a donkey 50, but these probably represent record ages, as 25 to 40 years is a good life-span for these animals.

The domestic dog is usually old at from 12 to 15, but sometimes doubles those figures. My daily newspaper has just recorded an Irish terrier of 28 years of age. The domestic cat also occasionally exceeds 20 years. A rabbit may reach 10, and a mouse 6 years.

Birds, such as the parrot, golden eagle, swan and the raven, sometimes exceed a century, while both the goose and the duck may reach 50 years. Such birds as the thrush and robin are old at 12 years.

[*Wide World Photos.*

Size does not necessarily indicate long life, the elephant living but little longer than Man, but he may live to be over a hundred.

Carp and pike are amongst the centenarians of fishes, but in contrast to these are the European Transparent Goby and the Ice-fish of China, both of which are said to live for only one year—a feature that is unique in vertebrates.

Reptiles and amphibians attain still greater ages. The crocodile is said to reach 200 years, and Lord Rothschild once had a giant tortoise stated to be over 300 years old. A slow-worm may live for 30 years, and newts and toads for 40 years.

[E.N.A.

THE EXTRAORDINARY FOUR-FACED TOWERS OF THE ANCIENT TEMPLE
OF BAYON, ANGKOR THOM.

There are fifty of the towers, all with a face of Brahma on each of their four sides. It was meant that no one should ever lose sight of that mysterious face.

153

THE GREAT TEMPLE AT ANGKOR-VAT, CAMBODIA, NOW RECLAIMED
FROM THE JUNGLE.

SPLENDOURS OF THE PAST ONCE MORE REVEALED

A LITTLE more than a thousand years ago, in the heart of Cambodia, there reigned a line of rich and mighty kings. But we must remember where Cambodia is. If we travelled eastward from India, we should come to Burmah, then to Siam, and on the east of that state to Cambodia, which is a protectorate of France in what is called Indo-China. In that land the kings built palaces and temples of great splendour. In time these kings died, their kingdom decayed and their wonderful city and its temples were overgrown by the forest. We must always remember that unless man fights the forest and the jungle, they come back and slowly hide or eat away all his proud works. But to-day the jungle has been cleared away and these splendid buildings have been brought back to the light.

In the forest north of a great lake, the traveller comes upon the town of Angkor and the temple of Angkor-Vat. They stand in a rectangular space, two miles in each direction. The temple of Bayon, which we see in the picture, with its famous four-faced towers, was built for the worship of Brahma, but afterwards the people changed their religion, and the temple was then given up to the religion of Buddha.

The temple stood in an enclosure with long galleries. At the centre rose a high tower on a circular base. In that temple there are fifty towers with a face of Brahma on each of their four sides; these towers line the galleries. It was meant that no one should ever lose sight of that mysterious face.

It is not only in the ancient stones that this kingdom and its temple lives. There are still ceremonies and dances which are still performed even to-day before the ruins of the temple.

In the East no one would be surprised to find that these dances had not changed in any material way since the days when proud kings built these temples and palaces to last, as they thought, for all time.

[Dorien Leigh.

ONE OF THE EXTRAORDINARY AND GIGANTIC STATUES AT ANGKOR.

They are only ruins now, but splendid ruins. And the old days are not altogether forgotten.

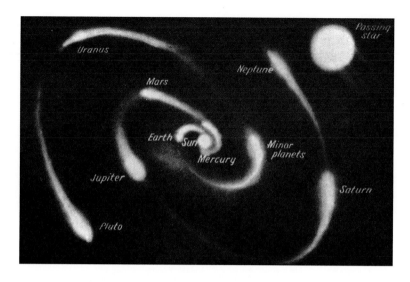

THE BIRTH OF THE EARTH AND THE PLANETS.

It is thought that æons ago a big body, a star probably, passed so close to the Sun that its gravity-pull drew a tremendous " tooth " from it—a great whirling, tooth-shaped streamer of fiery gas three or four thousand million miles in length. As this cooled, it would condense into " drops "—now the planets of the Solar System.

WHEN THE EARTH WAS BORN

" Science truly understood, is not the death, but the birth, of mystery, awe and reverence."—*Professor T. G. Donnan.*

FOR ages men wondered how old the Earth was and tried to find out, without ever suspecting that Nature had herself provided at least one most excellent clue to this much-longed-for secret—radio-active substances. These substances are not made of ordinary atoms but of live and luminous ones which keep breaking up and changing into other atoms quite automatically with the mere lapse of time. Uranium, a very heavy metal, is one of the three or four primary or parent radio-active elements and it explodes at regular intervals, shooting out as it does so, an atom of a light gas called helium. *After each expulsion of a helium atom, an entirely new substance is formed.* When an atom of uranium has shot off three atoms of helium, it becomes an atom of radium—a name so famous that it hardly needs an introduction here. This wonderful transmutation of elements (the changing of one

156

element into another) is a marvel which even to-day only Nature can perform. Radium, too, fires off atoms, breaks up and turns into something else till there is no radio-active substance left at all, but only lead and helium gas. All other radio-active elements do the same. In every case, the final end of this astonishing, mysterious process is helium and lead ; lead, however, which is just a shade lighter than ordinary lead and can therefore be distinguished by its weight. Now, in minute traces, radio-active substances are found in all rocks the world over and the rate at which they turn into lead and helium has

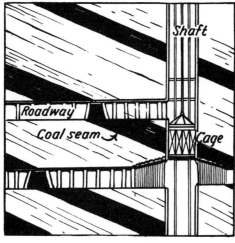

SHAFT AND GALLERIES IN A COALMINE.

Showing the coal seams, in this case tilted, between strata of other rock. The principal coal seams of England began to form not less than two hundred million years ago.

been successfully measured by years of careful experiments. One of the first substances to be analysed, a piece of rock from Ceylon, contained 286 million times more helium than the included radio-active fragment could generate in a year. These particular Ceylon rocks, therefore, must be at least 286 million years old. And they are among the more newly-formed ones of the Earth's crust. Each different geologic age has its own distinctive series of rock-strata formed under different physical conditions from the ruins and sediments of previous ones. The oldest known rocks, such as

black mica and Canadian pegmatite, are shown to be about 1200 million years old. Pitchblende, one of the chief radium-bearing ores, has been mined at St. Ives, Cornwall, and an examination of specimens tells us that the principal coal seams of England began to form not less than 200 million years ago. The presence of radio-active elements in the older rocks is often betrayed by tiny, shining spots of great beauty called pleochroic haloes. These consist of the accumulating atoms of helium fired off by the various radio elements. Since they are fired off equally in all directions, they accumulate in a circular or spherical-shaped shell surrounding the still tinier central speck of radium or uranium. Pleochroic haloes are never larger than about 1/650th part of an inch in diameter and their colour deepens so slowly (the helium accumulates so slowly) that hundreds of millions of years are usually needed for them to become noticeable even to the trained eye. That is why hardly any have been discovered in the newer, younger rocks.

Perhaps the chief value of the radio-active method of telling the age of the Earth is that the rate of decay of these substances seems to be absolutely fixed and unalterable. If the rate varied with circumstances or from time to time without any reason, then, of course, this method would be of little or no use. If a watch behaved like this—if it gained one day, lost the next day, and perhaps stopped occasionally altogether, we should throw it aside as useless. The radium clock of geology, however, seems to be as regular and reliable as sunrise. Even greater extremes of physical and chemical conditions, of heat and cold and pressure, than normally prevail in Nature have failed to stop or hinder the working of its wonderful micro-machinery. One scientist subjected it to temperatures ranging from 300° *below* zero (Fahrenheit) to 3000° *above* zero. No effect whatsoever was produced. The precious radium clock also refused to take the slightest notice of a similar temperature plus a *terrific pressure of twelve tons to the square inch or*

ROCK-STRATA IN THE DIFFERENT AGES AND THE CREATURES THAT THEN INHABITED THE EARTH.

Each Geologic Age has its own distinctive rock-strata, formed under different physical conditions from the ruins and sediments of previous ones.

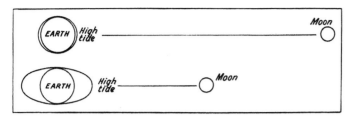

THE MOON'S GRAVITY ATTRACTION PRODUCES THE TIDES.

If the Moon came twice as near to us as she now is, the primary tides would be eight-fold greater, as shown in the above diagram.

2000 *times the average atmospheric pressure at sea-level.* Nothing at all seems able to speed it up or slow it down in the least degree. To-day, most scientists believe that the Earth and her sister planets of the solar system were originally part of the Sun. All bodies possess a mysterious attraction for all other bodies ; this is known as gravity or gravitation (see the article relating to Weight, page 197). This mutual attraction varies according to the bigness and distance apart of the bodies concerned. The Moon's gravity attraction for the Earth is the chief agency that produces the tides. It causes the ocean waters to bunch up beneath the overhead Moon ; they are lifted up directly towards her to the extent of two to three feet. If, however, the Moon came twice as near to us as she now is, the primary tides would be eight-fold greater. *In the Bay of Fundy they would be* 800 *feet high.* Now the Moon is but a small astronomical body eighty times lighter than the Earth. Were she eighty times *heavier* than the Earth, what would the tides be like ? That, I think, can safely be left to our imaginations.

Similarly, then, a big body, a star probably, is thought to have once passed so close to the Sun that its gravity-pull not only raised mighty tides on the Sun's flaming surface, but actually drew a tremendous " tooth " from it—a great tooth-shaped streamer of fiery gas three or four thousand million miles in length. As this cooled amid the iciness of space, it would condense into astronomical " drops," much as a rain cloud condenses into separate rain

INNER STRUCTURE OF THE EARTH.

The solid black is the centrosphere or heavy central core of nickel-iron. This merges into the intermediate zone of mixed stone and metal. The black arc at the top is the lithosphere or outer crust, forty-five miles or so thick.

drops. The " astro-drops," as we may perhaps describe them here, are now the planets of the solar system. All the planets rotate or spin round on their axes because they were endowed with this motion at their birth by their parent, the great Sun, which itself rotates. They one and all travel round the Sun in the same direction—the direction, of course, in which the wandering starry stranger, their other parent, passed by the Sun millions of years ago. Thus in the solar system there is one-way traffic only. Our little Earth really moves in more than six different directions at once : (1) on her axis once in every twenty-four hours: (2) round the Sun once in every $365\frac{1}{4}$ days; (3) round the common centre of gravity of the Earth-Moon system; (4) towards the star *Vega* in the constellation *Lyra* at twelve miles per second; (5) round the centre or hub of the Galaxy at 200 miles a second ; (6) its axis of rotation wanders round a circle roughly 26 feet in diameter every 430 days. This means that the North Pole is always 26 feet from where it was $7\frac{1}{2}$ months ago. This motion is due to the enormous strain of vibration set up by her other rapid motions. The Earth's axis describes a great circle in the sky every 26,000 years or so. This is similar to the

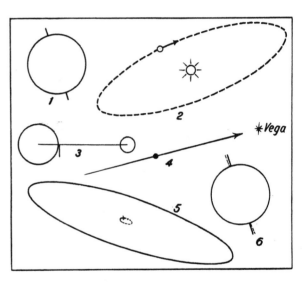

THE EARTH MOVES IN MORE THAN SIX DIFFERENT DIRECTIONS AT ONCE.

(1) On her axis once in every twenty-four hours. (2) Round the Sun once in every $365\frac{1}{4}$ days. (3) Round the common centre of gravity of the Earth-Moon system. (4) Towards the star *Vega* at twelve miles per second. (5) Round the centre of the Galaxy at 200 miles a second. (6) The Earth's axis of rotation wanders round a circle roughly 26 feet in diameter every 430 days. The axis also describes a great circle in the sky every 26,000 years or so.

swaying or wobbling of a top that is " asleep," or spinning very fast.

The Earth consists of materials which, on the whole, are approximately five and a half times heavier than water. The rocks of her crust, as far down as men have been able to go, are only about two and three-quarter times as heavy as water. Mother Earth must have a very heavy central core, therefore, probably as is now believed, made of highly-compressed nickel-iron seven or eight or even twelve times heavier than water (see diagram.) This fits in splendidly with the current theory of her molten origin. The great heat of her childhood days would separate the heavy metallic stuff from the lighter stony or rocky materials just as the heat of the smelting furnace separates the iron from the slag. Before solidifying, the heavy nickel-iron would sink down towards the centre, while the light, slaggy stuff would rise up to the top and form the rocks of the outer crust. This crust is estimated to be about 45 miles thick, and the heavy central core 5000 miles in diameter. The intermediate zone is believed to be about 1400 miles thick, or deep, and to consist of mixed iron and stone, lighter than the core, yet heavier than the thin outer crust.

THE BOMBARDIER BEETLE

HERE is a tiny Bombardier Beetle actually emitting with explosive force from the rear portion of its body, the powerful acrid fluid (from which it gets its name) to drive off a large predacious Ground Beetle, which thought it saw in the smaller insect an easy victim. Not content with a single explosion, the Bombardier Beetle emits several ejections in approved quick-fire fashion and successfully drives off its enemies. Several species of beetles, some ants and other insects possess this extraordinary power of protection, which is somewhat similar to the means adopted by the skunk in the animal kingdom.

[H. Bastin.

A Bombardier Beetle chased by a large predacious Ground Beetle, which it is " bombarding.'

WHY HE IS CALLED THE "BUTCHER BIRD"

THE Red-backed Shrike, or Butcher Bird, is a regular visitor to the British Isles, arriving in May and departing in September. The nest is usually situated in the heart of a stout thorn bush, and the name Butcher Bird is derived from the bird's habit of impaling its captured prey on the thorns of a neighbouring bush, which is known as the "larder." The young are fed very rapidly and the food varies from field mice, beetles, moths and spiders, down to bumble bees—an enormous quantity of the last named. Totally indigestible matter such as bones from the mice, and legs and hard wing casings from beetles, are ejected by the young birds in the form of pellets measuring one and a quarter inches in length and nearly half an inch in diameter. At the nest shown, in a total period of ten hours during which observation was kept, 179 visits were made by the two birds, 109 by the female and 70 by the male.

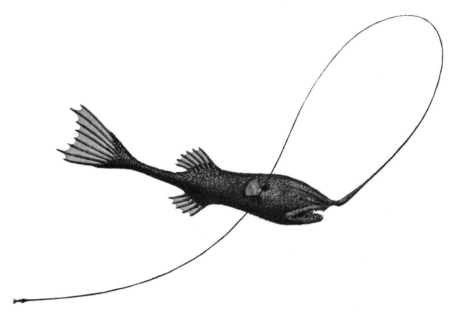

OCEANIC ANGLER-FISH (*GIGANTACTIS MACRONEMA*).

The long fishing-line attached to the snout ends in a luminous lure to attract inquisitive fish within reach of the huge jaws.

NIGHTMARE DENIZENS OF AN UNEXPLORED WORLD

SOME parts of the oceans are so deep that Mount Everest could be sunk in them and completely submerged. In these " deeps," as they are called, is a world of perpetual night, since the last rays of light can penetrate only to about two thousand feet, and perpetual winter, since the temperature falls rapidly the deeper one goes. The great depth of water presses with a terrific force on everything immersed in it. At a depth of three thousand five hundred feet, the pressure would be nearly one ton per square inch. The pressure of steam in the boiler of a steam locomotive would be about two hundred and fifty pounds per square inch (only about one ninth of the pressure of the water at a depth of three thousand and five hundred feet). It seems unbelievable that any live creature could exist under such conditions, but we now know that many weird and strange forms of animal life do live there in this almost unexplored world.

Some of them look almost like things seen in a nightmare, but they are by nature well fitted for the kind of life they are forced to lead. Some of them have developed large eyes with which to catch faint glimmers of light. Others have poor eyes or are totally blind and have developed a very delicate sense of touch instead, just as a blind man would. These latter fish have grown specially long and sensitive feelers, with which they grope their way about the ocean deeps.

Many deep-sea fish have light-producing organs on their heads and bodies. The whole body may be covered with a

luminous slime, or more elaborate light-producing organs with a lens and a reflector like headlamps or torches may be developed. The light produced varies in colour from a vivid greenish phosphorescent glow to shades of orange, purple and blue. In some fish the light organs are arranged in definite patterns, glistening like jewels, or resembling the illuminated port-holes of a liner at night, thus helping in all probability other fish of the same kind to recognise each other and keep together in a shoal. The deep-sea Anglers have lights on the ends of long, slender rod-like structures growing from their heads, which serve as fishing-lines and bait to lure inquisitive fish within reach of the huge jaws of the lurking Anglers.

A DEEP-SEA ANGLER (*Melanocetus niger*).
Perhaps because food is comparatively scarce in the deeps, the inhabitants often appear to be all head and mouth, with very little body.

Perhaps due to the fact that food is comparatively scarce in the deeps, the inhabitants often appear to be all head and mouth, with very little body. The flexible jaws beset with fierce, sharp-pointed teeth, are able to gape open widely, and the body can stretch to an enormous extent to hold a meal which may be several times larger than the diner itself. The captured fish is quickly swallowed whole, so that there is no chance of escape, and there is no likelihood of having to share the meal with others. After a meal of such dimensions the fish settles down quietly to enjoy it, which process probably occupies a period of several days. A Gulper once swallowed a fish three times its own length, and nearly ten times its weight, but the meal was more than it could manage and caused it to float helplessly to the surface, where it was discovered.

[*British Museum (Nat. Hist)*.

ANOTHER OCEANIC ANGLER-FISH (*LINOPHRYNE ARBORIFER*).

Note the size of the mouth and the teeth. The flexible jaws are able to gape open widely, and the body can stretch to an enormous extent to hold a meal, maybe several times larger than the diner itself. The long beard is probably luminous.

A specimen from the Hudson Gorge with Turquoise-tinted scales.

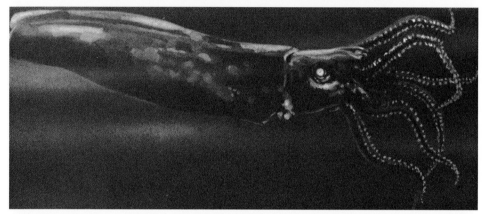

A Squid with five thousand luminous portholes.

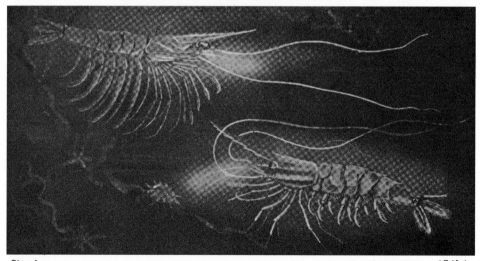

Photos]   [*E.N.A.*
Two deep-sea prawns (*Aristeus* and *Heterocarpus*) which have the faculty of pouring out clouds of luminous fluid, serving, perhaps, like the ink of the cuttle-fish, to baffle pursuers.

NIGHTMARE DENIZENS OF THE DEEP.

WHAT ARE WE MADE OF ?

THIS is a very simple First Form question, but it is one that quickly leads into the wonderland of physical science. The biology text-books tell us what our bodies are made of ; i.e. over 50 % water, with smaller percentages of fat, sugar, albumen and salts. It is also funny to think that there are over twenty different minerals in the average healthy human being, including iron, copper, zinc and traces of the rare and familiar metals, gold and silver.

Fig. 1. A molecule of water with its three atoms, two of hydrogen and one of oxygen.

That, however, is only part of the story. The most strange and important part is yet to come. Science has now shown that everything in the world, dead and alive, without a single exception, is composed of separate little specks or units called atoms. They are inconceivably tiny, far, far too tiny ever to be seen by mortal eyes, no matter how powerful a microscope we may use to help us. That is one reason why men have been so long in discovering them. Atoms are really the ultimate little bricks with which Nature has built the entire Universe, suns and planets, mice and men, trees and stones alike. Science has found, further, that in no case whatsoever are the atom-bricks of an object actually touching each other. They are always held apart by some mysterious, electric-like force. They always keep one another at arm's length, so to speak, and the distance between them, which varies widely, decides whether a thing (substance) is light or heavy. When close together they make a thing heavy like lead ; when far apart they make a thing light like gas and air and cork. The distance between the atoms is, in proportion to their size, enormous. *In those heaviest substances on Earth, where they are most crowded together, the atoms are still (relatively) farther apart than the Earth, the Moon and Mars.* The astonishing smallness and spacing of atoms may, perhaps, be best imagined from the following simple facts :

There are 1000 million million million million (1 followed by 27 noughts) atoms in a man's body, and if they could all be

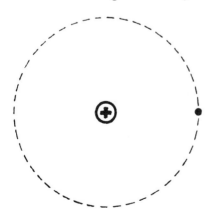

Fig. 2. An atom of hydrogen (nucleus and one electron).

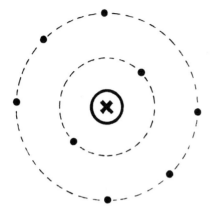

Fig. 3. An atom of oxygen (eight electrons and the nucleus).

brought together in contact, *the man would become a mere speck barely visible without a magnifying glass.* The spaces separating the atoms are generally described as pores, and it has been estimated, too, that if the globe we live on were absolutely without pores (that is, if there were no spaces between the atoms composing it), *the whole Earth would be shrunk to no bigger than a tennis ball.* If boys and girls were as little as atoms, stone walls and steel doors would appear to be full of gaping holes through which they would be able to pass as easily as a fly goes through wire mesh.

When you ask, then, " What am I Made of ? " Science answers gravely, " Mostly holes—myriads of tiny, invisible holes." The actual substance in all things does not amount to one-thousandth part of their size and extent. More than 99 % of ourselves and the Universe consists of what, thoughtlessly, we call sheer emptiness—what most of us look upon as nothingness. To-day, however, Science knows better. Space is NOT " waste " space at all, NOT nothingness. How can it be when over 99 % of you and I and the world is built of it, and without it, none would be what they are ?

We are slowly realising to our surprise and bewilderment, that space is one of Nature's greatest and subtlest creations. Sir James Jeans has likened the whole Universe to a soap-bubble. The Universe-bubble, however, is not blown of soap and water, but of " empty space welded onto empty time."

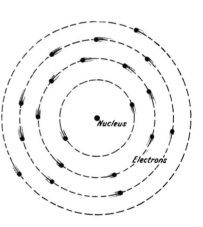

Fig. 4. An atom of calcium (twenty electrons and the nucleus).

A MOTHER BAT AND HER BABY.   [*Dorien Leigh.*
The young one is carried like this even when the mother is in flight.

AND BABY GOES TOO!

AUSTRALIAN mammals always carry their new-born babies with them, generally hiding them in a big pocket of skin which grows on the front of the mother's body. Their young are not long-legged, furry creatures, like lambs or calves, but look more like little pinkish caterpillars, with tiny stumps for their arms and legs, and a new-born Great Grey Kangaroo is so small that three of them will fit into an ordinary match box without any difficulty ! So unless the mother keeps such a tiny baby somewhere safe, she will certainly lose it. A young kangaroo grows fur, and long legs and tail, when it is about four months old, and for the next few weeks can be seen looking out of its mother's pocket and eating grass while she has her meals off leaves and bushes. It soon begins to climb out of the pocket and play with other " Joeys," as the baby kangaroos are called in Australia, though it rushes back to its mother at any alarm, and in its hurry often falls into her pouch head first ! Big kangaroos can move very fast by leaps of many yards ; in fact, the mother Red Kangaroo is called the " Flying Doe." The Joey is often too heavy to be carried in an emergency, and if a mother kangaroo is chased by an enemy, she first pulls the baby out of her pocket and puts it under a hedge or bush; then if she escapes she comes back to look for it when the danger is over.

Some pouched animals, such as the Tasmanian Devil, move on all fours instead of upright, and kill sheep and poultry and any other creatures they can overpower. They have their pockets opening backwards, and carry their babies tail first, so that their heads look out at the back! Others, that live in trees, like the Koala or Native

A KOALA, OR AUSTRALIAN NATIVE BEAR, CARRYING ITS BABY ON ITS BACK.

This quaint little animal feeds principally on the shoots and buds of eucalyptus trees. Was he the original Teddy Bear?

AND BABY GOES TOO!

Bear, keep their babies in the pocket for a shorter time, and after about three months the very attractive and friendly baby is carried clinging to its mother's back, while she climbs about eucalyptus trees eating the leaves.

In America there are pouched animals called opossums living in forests and sometimes on the roofs of houses. They are smaller than cats, with long, sharp snouts, and they can take hold of things with hands, feet, and tail, for they have " thumbs " and " fingers," instead of paws and claws. Opossums sleep in hollow trees by day, and hunt for

[*Fox Photos.*

A WALLABY AND HER YOUNG.
The baby soon begins to climb out of the pocket and play with other youngsters, though it rushes back to its mother when alarmed.

food at night, eating birds, squirrels, eggs, fruit, and even rubbish from gutters if nothing else is available. The young are born very small and helpless, like baby kangaroos, and live shut up in their mother's pouch until they are about a fortnight old. An opossum may have ten or twelve babies at once, instead of a single one like the kangaroo, and soon they grow too big for the pouch and have to climb out on to their mother's back. They hold on by twisting their tails round hers and look like tiny strap-hangers. In many kinds of opossum, as soon as

[*D. Seth Smith.*

TASMANIAN DEVILS.
These animals kill sheep and poultry and any other creatures they can overpower.

the first family is old enough to be carried this way, a new litter of babies is born, so that one mother opossum may have to carry twenty or more young ones, some on her back and some in her pocket. No wonder, then, that she moves rather slowly, and if chased by people and dogs, pretends to be dead, in order to be left alone !

Bats spend all day hanging up-side down from the big claws in their toes, and as the mother bat makes no sort of nest for her baby, young bats have to hang as well, but they cling to the fur on the front of their mother's body instead of to twigs or ledges. Then at sunset, when bats leave their resting places in hollow trees or old buildings or caves, and dart about, catching moths and gnats and other insects to eat, the babies are taken as well. Fortunately they are very strong flyers, and can avoid all obstacles in the dark, not by seeing them, but because they can feel the nearness of even tiny objects like threads or twigs before they touch them. In this way, also by their keen ears, bats can catch insects which would be invisible to us in the dark. Sometimes they catch a big moth or beetle which cannot be gobbled up at once ; then the bat bends its tail forward to make a little pocket, pushes its catch

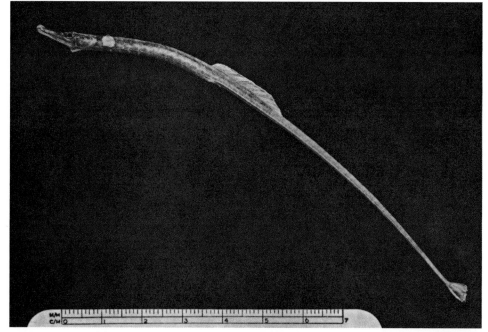

[H. Bastin.

A PIPE FISH.
The father Pipe Fish has a groove on the under side of his body and tail, with flaps of skin which can close over it, and the mother lays her eggs in this pocket. Even when the young fish have hatched and are old enough to start swimming about alone, they return to the pouch as soon as danger threatens.

in this and tucks its head down to chew it at leisure. All this happens while the bat goes on flying !

Young apes and monkeys cling to their mothers for a time, and are carried about from branch to branch through forests while their parents are hunting for food, and when the mother goes to sleep at night she takes the baby to bed with her. Chimpanzees spend a good deal of time on the ground, sometimes standing upright, otherwise running on all fours, but they climb up trees quickly and easily to find fruit and leaves and small animals for food. They build themselves little platforms of sticks each day, on one of the lower branches of a tree, and here they sleep at night and rest when they are tired. Each chimpanzee builds its own sleeping platform, but the mothers share theirs with their young for some months.

Some cold-blooded animals like fish also carry their young about. In a thin, long, green fish, called the Pipe Fish, the father has a groove on the under side of his body and tail, with flaps of skin which can close over it, and the mother lays her eggs in this pocket. They hatch here in safety, and the young remain with their father for some time. Even when they are old enough to leave him and start swimming about alone, as soon as any danger threatens, he opens his pouch for them to come back again. Unlike the mother kangaroo, he will do his best to escape carrying all the family with him! Pipe Fishes live round the Atlantic coasts, most of them in warm, weedy places like those off the coast of Florida or the south of Spain.

[*By Ewing Galloway, N.Y.*

A MOTHER OPOSSUM AND YOUNG.
The young live shut up in their mother's pouch until they are about a fortnight old, but soon they grow too big and have to climb out on to their mother's back. They hold on by twisting their tails round hers and look like tiny strap-hangers.

WHERE A MAN WOULD WEIGH 2,000 TONS

MARVELS AND MYSTERIES OF GRAVITATION

HERE we have another most elementary question, to which Science returns a most remarkable answer. "Your weight," says science, "may be almost anything or even nothing at all. *It all depends upon where you are weighed.*" You see, weight is simply a consequence of gravity or gravitation, the law of gravitation being one of the most fundamental and far-reaching in the whole realm of Nature. Every material object and particle, whatever its size, atom or nebula, dead or alive,

possesses a mysterious attractive property called gravity or gravitational attraction, which tends to pull all other material objects and particles towards it. Now the strength of this gravity-pull or attractive force depends only upon the quantity of stuff the object contains (its mass or tonnage) and how far you are away from it. A big thing, like a big man, has a stronger pull than a little one and the further you get away from either the weaker does the pull become.

"Weight and attraction are one and the same thing," said the famous French astronomer, Flammarion. "Our globe may be regarded as an immense mag-

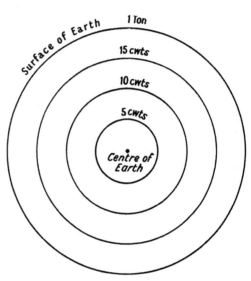

A TON DOES NOT ALWAYS WEIGH A TON.

Gravity steadily decreases from the surface to the centre of the Earth. Diagram shows what a ton of coal would weigh at 1,000, 2,000 and 3,000 miles below the surface. The centre of the Earth is approximately 4,000 miles below the surface, where our ton of coal would weigh *nothing*.

netic ball whose attraction holds us at its surface." In everyday life, the only gravity-pull that counts is the Earth's, because the Earth contains millions of times more stuff (substance) than any other object in our neighbourhood.

The nearest other body of any comparable size and mass is the Moon, about a quarter of a million miles away. A further point to remember is that gravity is strongest at the *surface* of a body. If, for example, you leave the Earth's surface, gravity becomes less and therefore your weight becomes less, *whether you go up or down, above or below*. You weigh a trifle less sitting in the circle of a theatre than you do in the stalls, because, of course, you are a trifle away from (above) the Earth's surface in the circle, while you actually are on it in the stalls. The amount of the reduction is very small for distances of a few feet like the above, but it has nevertheless been accurately measured by physicists. In fact, there are chemical balances so delicate that different results are obtained *when the weights are placed side by side and then one on top of another*. Moreover, for bigger distances, variations in weight become startling, almost fantastic. A ton of coal would weigh only 15 cwts., three-quarters of a ton, a thousand miles below the surface. It would weigh only half a ton two thousand miles below, and at the centre of the Earth, just under four thousand miles from the surface, *it would weigh nothing at all*. And if some good fairy or magician transported *you* there, neither would you. At the precise centre of gravity, nothing and nobody whatever has any weight whatever. Whatever weight you may possess elsewhere becomes zero and vanishes completely at this unique, inaccessible spot—the centre of the Earth, or of any other material object. Here you are surrounded equally on all sides by the material of the Earth, which pulls at you equally on all sides. Because you are pulled equally (with equal force) in *all* directions, you are pulled in *none*. No pull is exerted upon you because the countless contrary pulls cancel one another out ; they defeat their own ends as it were, and no pull means no weight. The old maxim speaks of too many cooks spoiling the broth. In this case, too many cooks have resulted in there being no broth at all. Even *on* the Earth's surface, however, you would weigh differently in scores of different places, because the Earth is not perfectly round and spherical but only roughly so, and its surface is not thence always at exactly the same distance from its centre—the centre of gravity. The Earth is flattened a little round the poles and bulges out a little round the equator. Hence your weight would be a little heavier at the North Pole than it is in England, because the North Pole is six or seven miles *nearer* the Earth's centre than London is, and gravity is proportionately stronger there. In this case, the difference is not so insignificant by any means. A twelve-stone Englishman would weigh six or seven ounces more at the North Pole. He would also weigh six or seven ounces *less* at the equator because the equator is six or seven miles *further from* the Earth's centre than London is, and gravity is necessarily so much weaker there in consequence.

We all know that the Moon is chiefly responsible for the tides. It is her gravity-pull which produces them. Now the weight of everything and every person varies according to the varying distance and position of the Moon in the sky. Is it not astonishing to realise that between the time when the Moon is directly over her head and when it sets on her horizon, the tonnage (or weight) of the " Queen Mary " has altered by no less than thirty pounds, over two stone! *Just think of it! As you watch our silvery little satellite mounting higher and*

MOON OVERHEAD
20 lb. lighter

MOON ON HORIZON
10 lb. heavier

"Queen Mary"

As you watch our silvery little satellite, the Moon, mounting higher and higher above you, your weight is becoming less and less—you are getting lighter. In the case of the " Queen Mary," she would be 20 lbs. lighter with the Moon directly overhead and when the Moon is on the horizon, 10 lbs. heavier.

higher above you in the night sky, your weight is becoming less and less— you are getting lighter and lighter. In climbing the sky towards the zenith (that point of the heavens straight above your head) the Moon is steadily getting a more effective, direct gravity grip upon you, which reaches its maximum when it is immediately overhead. Then, it is pulling in direct opposition to Mother Earth, and counteracts the pull of the Earth, to the extent of twenty pounds in the case of the " Queen Mary."

When we leave the Earth altogether, however, and visit other worlds, perhaps the most remarkable discoveries of all await us. *A ton of coal would weigh twenty-seven tons on the Sun.* A man weighing eleven stone here would find himself weighing three hundred and twenty stone at the Sun's surface.

By way of sensational contrast, let us now go and visit what astronomers call the asteroids. These are a large swarm of tiny little bodies, baby worlds if you like, which revolve round the Sun between the well-known planets, Mars and Jupiter. They might almost be described as the dwarfs and pigmies of the planetary family. Ceres is the name of the largest one and it is only 480 miles in diameter, as against the Earth's diameter of nearly 8000 miles. Its surface gravity is thirty-five times weaker than our globe's, and an average man, going to Ceres for a holiday, would find himself a mere four or five pounds heavy, or perhaps light, we should rather say. He would bounce about there as a ping-pong ball does here, and be able easily to jump one hundred feet high.

If, now, in conclusion, we leave our own little solar system behind us and strike out into the remoter depths of space, we shall, I think, find it well worth while. We should find a few stars called " white dwarfs," white because they are white in colour, and dwarfs because they are so small in size or bulk. They are made of the densest, heaviest material in the entire known Universe. Some unknown catastrophic process has squeezed their substance to an extent utterly beyond adequate description or comprehension. Could he exist there, a man on their surface would weigh *over* 2000 *tons*, so inconceivably strong and terrific is their gravity-pull.

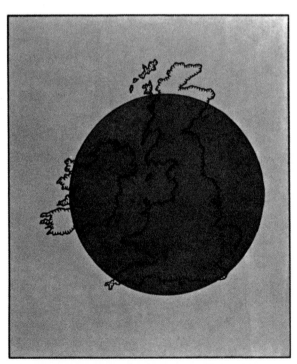

Comparative sizes of British Isles and Ceres, the largest " pocket planet," or asteroid, which is 480 miles in diameter. A twelve-year-old girl on Ceres would weigh only about 2lbs.

FUNGI FORMING "A FAIRY RING." [H. Bastin.

THE
PLANT'S CHEMICAL LABORATORY

IN order to explain the chemical activities of plants in general we can take as an example a common plant such as the Buttercup. The first thing that is noticed about the plant, apart from its yellow flower, is that it has green leaves and stem. This colour is due to the presence of a green substance known as chlorophyll, which is indispensable for the formation of food materials in the leaf. As the sun shines on the leaf some of the rays, notably the blue and the violet, are absorbed by the chlorophyll and the energy obtained is used by the leaf to make food from carbon-dioxide and water. The carbon-dioxide is one of the constituents of air and passes into the leaf through minute openings (*stomata*) in the lower surface, and thence through the thin walls of the cells containing chlorophyll. The gas is then split up and combined with the water obtained by the roots to form a sugar. This chemical action is known as photosynthesis.

The chemical processes involved in this building up of food materials, such as sugar from carbon-dioxide and water, are not fully understood. No one has yet succeeded in making sugar from those

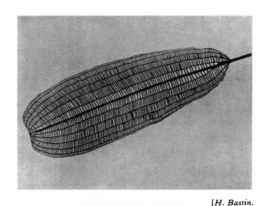

A LATTICE LEAF. [H. Bastin.

This is aquatic, and one of the most remarkable of all leaves.

two substances in a chemical laboratory. It is known that light is essential to the process, since it is concerned with the absorption of the rays of the sun. If the Buttercup is placed in a dark room, it will grow for a short time but all new leaves will be quite white and therefore unable to make food, and the plant will soon die. If it is taken out of the dark room while still alive and exposed to the light, the white leaves will soon turn green. Chlorophyll cannot be manufactured by the plant in the dark, neither will the plant manufacture food materials, even if chlorophyll is present.

Another important chemical process in the life of a plant is that of respiration. Just as animals must breathe in order to release the energy stored up in the food they consume, so plants must do likewise. The plant takes in oxygen through the stomata in the leaves, uses it to break down the food materials, and energy is released, carbon-dioxide and water are produced as waste products. It can be seen, then, that respiration is the opposite of photosynthesis. In the latter, the energy of the sun's rays is used to build up food materials from simple substances ; in the former, the food materials are broken down and energy is released, which is used in the growth of the plant.

Plants which do not possess chlorophyll obtain their food materials by living on other plants as parasites ; examples of this are the Broomrapes and Dodder. Others, such as the Fungi, live on the dead remains of plants or animals, and are also without green colouring matter.

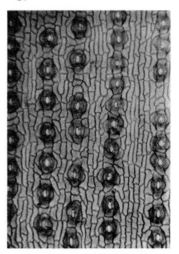

[John J. Ward.

Breathing pores on the leaf of the Monkey Puzzle Tree (*Araucaria imbricata*), greatly enlarged.

AN AMERICAN TOAD WITH ITS THROAT PUFFED OUT WHILE SERENADING HIS LADY-LOVE.

CURIOUS WAYS OF BREATHING

WHEN we need a good breath of air, the respiratory centre of the brain instructs the muscles to contract and expand the chest. Then about a pint of additional air enters the lungs.

The air passes through the nostrils to the back of the mouth, and then through the windpipe, or trachea, as it is called, to the lungs. The trachea divides and spreads into each lung, forming a network of tubes. These tubes become finer and finer until an enormous internal area is produced. In man, it is estimated at about thirty times that of his body surface. The incoming air rushes over this huge surface, and the chest, in automatically assuming its former position, expels the exhausted air.

Such is the wonderful machinery that comes into action each time we breathe. Birds, though, have a still more complicated breathing mechanism. To their lungs is added a series of air-sacs, and these again communicate with air-filled cavities in their bones. These additional air-sacs assist the bird when it is flying at great heights

[H. Bastin.

A Slug, showing the pulmonary aperture, or breathing hole, on the right edge of the " mantle," on the " shoulder."

in thin air, and also add to its buoyancy while in flight.

Fishes breathe by means of gills, which form a series of thin plates containing numerous blood vessels. Through these gill-plates oxygen is dissolved from the water that flows over them. There are fishes, though, which live in ponds and rivers that sometimes dry up, and these can breathe atmospheric air, which is stored in special reservoirs in their anatomy.

Frogs, toads, newts and other amphibians, breathe by means of gills in their tadpole stage, but, later, they develop lungs and become air-breathers to live on the land.

Insects breathe through a series of holes (spiracles) arranged in pairs along each side of the segments of the body. These spiracles provide the opening to a system of branching air-tubes (tracheæ) which spreads through the insect's whole anatomy, even to the tips of the feelers, and into the feet, no matter how small the insect may be.

Owing to this direct method of conveying air to their tissues, insects are not provided with lungs and blood vessels. Air is taken to their blood, instead of their blood going to the lungs for aeration, as in the case of the higher animals.

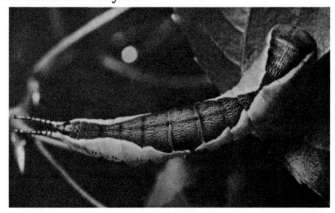

[Dorien Leigh.

Larva of a Puss Moth, showing, along the flank, the " spiracles " through which it breathes.

By courtesy of]   [*The High Commissioner for New Zealand.*

THE KIWI, OR APTERYX, NEW ZEALAND'S WINGLESS BIRD.

This bird is about the size of a fowl. It can hardly run at all, so spends all day asleep in its hole and creeps out to feed only at dusk.

BIRDS THAT CANNOT FLY

OSTRICHES, Emus, Cassowaries and Rheas are the biggest birds in the world, but as they have no stiff feathers and only very small wings, they are unable to fly, and have to trust to the speed of their long, strong legs to make their escape from enemies.

Ostriches live in sandy wastes or bushy districts in South Africa, and many of them are now kept on farms for the sake of the beautiful curled, white feathers which decorate the male ostriches' wings and tail. The rest of his body is covered with glossy black plumage, but his long, thin neck and his legs and feet are bare and show his bright pink skin. The female ostrich is a dull, dusky-brown colour all over. Ostriches run in very long strides, with their wings outstretched, and can go fast enough to overtake a galloping horse. They kick dangerously hard, and will also fight with their short, flat beaks. In the wilder parts of Africa small flocks of them often live with herds of zebra or antelope, eating much the same food, but swallowing hard objects like stones and nails, as well.

In South America Ostriches have some smaller relations, called R h e a s, or South American Ostriches, which are much the same shape, though they have no tail at all, and are covered with

By courtesy of]   [Carl Hagenbeck's Tierpark.

A COCK OSTRICH.

Showing the bird's beautiful plumes. Ostriches run in very long strides, with their wings outstretched, and can go fast enough to overtake a galloping horse.

[Carthew & Kinnaird.

A RHEA OR SOUTH AMERICAN OSTRICH.

Rheas have no tail at all, and are covered with soft, greyish-brown feathers.

soft, greyish-brown feathers. These are often used for making feather dusters.

Emus and Cassowaries live in the wilder parts of Australia and New Guinea ; the Emus in open, sandy country on the mainland, while Cassowaries are found in dense jungle, both in North Australia and New Guinea. The Emu's feathers are a dull, dark brown colour, and patches of the bird's bluish skin show through the thin down on its neck. It is a fast runner and can swim well,

[*Fox Photos.*

A COCK EMU with FIVE CHICKS.
Emus come from open, sandy country in the wilder parts of Australia and New Guinea.

Cassowaries are rather heavy runners, but are good at jumping over quite big obstacles, and they are always ready to fight, even among themselves.

Besides these big birds, there are also small flightless birds, about the size of hens, found in New Zealand, and called Kiwis. They can hardly run at all, so they spend all day asleep in their holes and creep out to feed only at dusk. They find their meals of worms and grubs by poking tree stumps with their long beaks and sniffing the ground. They are also helped to find food in the dark by long, sensitive hairs like cats' whiskers.

and it eats grass and berries and a few insects.

Cassowaries are much more brilliant and beautiful birds, with glossy black feathers, except on their bare necks, which are coloured blue, yellow, red, pink and white in patches ! They have smaller and sharper beaks than the other big birds, and at the back these grow into horny lumps, or helmets, on the top of the birds' heads to protect them while they are pushing their way through the jungle. They have four or five long, stiff black spines, as thick as pencils, growing along their tiny wings.

[*Carthew & Kinnaird.*

THE CASSOWARY.
The Cassowary has glossy black feathers and a brightly-coloured, bare neck. The " helmet " on top of the head protects the bird while pushing its way through the dense jungle, where it makes its home.

"MAN-MADE" PLANTS

AT first sight all the lettuces in a row look very much alike, one tomato plant looks just like the neighbouring one. In fact, it is not until we examine the plants more closely that we see that there are some differences, however small, between each lettuce plant. Some have larger leaves than others, some are different in shape, while there may be considerable variation in the size of the heart of each lettuce. It is the fact that no two plants of a kind are ever exactly alike that enables the plant-breeder to go to work. If he wants to obtain a variety with larger leaves, he selects the three or four plants with the largest leaves and allows them to grow to seed. The following year he sows the seed from these plants and from the seedlings he again chooses the plants with larger leaves to grow on to seed. After repeating this process for three or four years, he will finally have a variety of lettuce with very much larger leaves than his original plants. All the annual garden vegetables are grown from seeds which have been carefully selected for generations to obtain the most desirable characteristics. The common cabbage, Savoy cabbage, kale, Brussels sprouts, cauliflower and kohl-rabi are all descended from the wild cabbage (*Brassica oleracea*), which can be found growing wild on the chalky cliffs on the Dorset coast. The leaves of the first ancestor of the kale were probably only slightly more crinkly than were those of the ordinary wild cabbage. A gardener must have noticed it and saved the seeds from the plant and raised seedlings all with crinkly leaves. Careful selection through many generations eventually produced the familiar vegetable of to-day. The other cabbage forms must have arisen in much the same way ; the cauliflower is a modification of the inflorescence, the kohl-rabi and Brussels sprouts of the stem, and the Savoy of the leaves.

Selection is not the only means of producing new races or forms. Hybridization often produces results much more quickly. The crossing of two different species which grow in widely-separated countries and, therefore, have no opportunity of crossing naturally, may result in the production of many new forms. Crossing has played an important part in the development of the garden strawberry, the large-fruited varieties of which have only been produced during the last hundred years or so. The cultivation of the wild wood strawberry (*Fragaria vesca*) probably started during the fifteenth century and

Some examples of cultivated flowers, fruit and vegetables, and the wild forms from which they have been developed. Brussels sprouts, Kohl-rabi, Broccoli, Cauliflower, Curly Kale and the market-gardener's Cabbage are all derived from the Wild Cabbage, and the wonderful Japanese Chrysanthemum is nothing more than a " glorified " Oxe-eye Daisy.

Budding : removing the bud.

until the seventeenth century varieties of this species and another wild European kind, the Hautbois strawberry (*Fragaria elatior*), were the only forms known to cultivation. The fruits of these varieties had quite a distinct flavour and were much smaller than those of the strawberry of the present day. In the seventeenth century *Fragaria virginiana*, the wild strawberry of North America, was brought to this country. The fruit was small, scarlet, and rounded in shape, and about thirty varieties of this species were eventually grown. One variety, Little Scarlet, is still grown at the present time on account of its suitability for jam making. A fourth species, the Chilean or Pine strawberry (*Fragaria chiloensis*), was brought from South America in 1712. This kind has larger fruits than any of the others, but for about a hundred years little notice was taken of it on account of the poor colour and quality of its fruit. In 1806, however, a gardener by the name of Michael Keens began raising strawberries from seed. He eventually obtained several large-fruited varieties, from seedlings of the Chilean strawberry, which were very similar to those grown to-day. Other growers soon followed

Budding : opening the bark preparatory to inserting the bud.

Budding : the bud inserted and bound with raffia.

Keen's lead, and during the nineteenth century many varieties such as Royal Sovereign, Noble, and King of the Earlies, appeared, mainly the result of cross-breeding. Recent breeding experiments with the Chilean and the North American strawberries have shown that these two species are doubtless the parents of the modern garden strawberry.

Many new varieties of flowers and fruits have arisen as " bud-sports." For instance, a single branch of an apple-tree might bear fruit of a different shape or colour from that of the rest of the tree. This " bud-sport " can be multiplied by taking buds from the branch showing the variation, and grafting them on to other apple trees. In this way a large stock of the new variety can be obtained in quite a short time. The Crimson Bramley apple arose as a " bud-sport " on a tree of " Bramleys Seedling," and many varieties of plum have appeared in this way. The nectarine often appears as a sport on the peach, and branches of peach have occasionally been found on the nectarine. A large number of the variegated and cut-leaved forms of ornamental plants commenced as bud varieties and have been multiplied by " budding,"

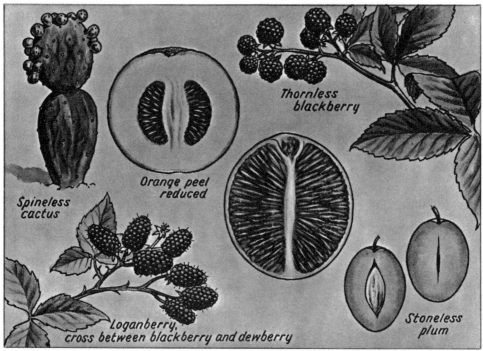

Thornless blackberry

Spineless cactus

Orange peel reduced

Loganberry, cross between blackberry and dewberry

Stoneless plum

FURTHER INSTANCES OF " IMPROVEMENT " TO SUIT MAN'S REQUIREMENTS.
The Orange has been made to provide more " flesh " and much less peel; the Plum can be almost stoneless; a Blackberry without thorns has been grown and a Cactus without spines.

usually because a good plant can be obtained very much more quickly by this method than from seed.

It sometimes happens that a new form or variety of some cultivated plant suddenly appears among an otherwise uniform batch of seedlings. We call this unexpected type of variation a " mutation." Double varieties of petunias, chrysanthemums, dahlias and many of our garden flowers have appeared suddenly in this way and have been improved by hybridization and selection. These mutations will usually breed true.

SAVAGE BUT FAITHFUL.
A tamed white wolf-dog guarding his sleeping master against his own savage ancestors.

190

A WILD CAT CATCHING FISH.

WHENCE CAME MAN'S ANIMAL FRIENDS ?

OUR domesticated animals present many puzzles as to their origin. The difficulty is that man has continually selected for breeding purposes variations that had some special appeal, until, to-day, we have in our kennels, stables, farmyards and aviaries, animals as unknown to wild nature as are some of the plants that may be found on the shelves in the greenhouse.

Notwithstanding the abnormal varieties that have been produced, they were all derived originally from some wild stock. Our various kinds of pigeons : the fantail, the jacobin, the homer, the tumbler, and other remarkable kinds, are all considered as descendants of the rock dove—a kind of wild pigeon that is still found in some of the seashore caves in Scotland and other parts of the British Isles. In producing these various breeds, during a few thousand years, Man has, as it were, speeded up evolution, and established types which would probably never have appeared in the ordinary sifting of natural selection.

It is the same with dogs. When at the dog show we see a St. Bernard beside a Pekinese, or a greyhound against a bulldog, it is difficult to realise that they are all supposed to be descendants of a few wolves and jackals of very uncertain species. The common European wolf is considered to be the chief ancestor of the dog, but neolithic

man, when using stone weapons, had his
dog, and since we have to go back to
prehistoric times, the problem becomes very
complex.

Our numerous kinds of domestic fowl are
undoubtedly descendants of the Indian or
Jungle Game Cock.

The domestic cat might seem to be a
descendant of the British wild cat—which is still
to be found in secluded places in Scotland—but
there is much evidence to show that it was
derived from the wild Caffre cat of Egypt.
We are, however, confronted with the same

INDIAN GAME COCK.

puzzling varieties as in the case of the
dog. There are the striped and tabby
types, the Manx tail-less cat, the beautiful
Angora, the familiar Persian and the
lynx-like Siamese.

These strange breeds derived from
species of many countries, and crossbred
continually, obviously do not admit of
any systematic classification where no
records are available.

BROWN LEGHORNS.

So we might take almost any of our
domestic animals, horses, cattle, and what
not, and meet with the same difficulty.

But when we find our dogs, with a
wolf origin, guarding and herding sheep,
we have to realise that the human factor
has played a wonderful part in animal
domestication—even though it has failed
really to tame the domestic cat.

The cat, though, is a nocturnal
animal, and we are far from knowing
all its mysterious movements when it
leaves home, or anything about its meals.
Often it may stay away for several days
together, and will then complacently walk
in as if nothing unusual had happened.

LIGHT SUSSEX.

A jungle game cock, the " Cock o' the Woods," killing with its spurs a fierce hawk which thought it saw in the game cock an easy victim.

TEETH IN STRANGE PLACES

MAN has normally thirty-two teeth, but the " wisdom teeth " do not always develop. That does not mean that people without those teeth will be less wise, for man, in the course of his evolution, is gradually losing his teeth. If we go back to monkeys, we find that some of these have thirty-six teeth, and, occasionally, a human being is found with that number.

The little Egg-eating Snake of South Africa presents a curious dental arrangement for a backboned animal. Its jaws are almost toothless, and it feeds on birds' eggs. Although its body is little thicker than a man's finger, yet it can swallow a pigeon's egg without difficulty.

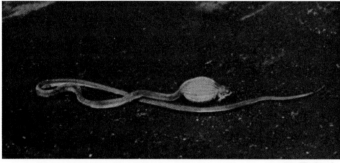

[F. W. Bond.

THE EGG-EATING SNAKE OF SOUTH AFRICA.

These snakes feed exclusively on birds' eggs. The one in the photograph has just swallowed one. The jaws are almost toothless, but in the gullet are about thirty " throat-teeth," really spines from the back-bone, which cut the egg-shell longitudinally into halves as it passes down the gullet.

When the egg has reached the gullet, it comes in contact with about thirty throat-teeth, which are really little spines from the joints of the vertebræ, or backbone, of the neck area, which penetrate the gullet. These strange backbone teeth cut the egg-shell longitudinally into halves. The contents are then absorbed, and the shell is disgorged. Strange to say, the halves of the empty shell are often found fitted together.

Some of the lower forms of life have remarkable chewing organs. While lobsters and crabs have six pairs of specialised jaws, yet their teeth are found in a strong framework in the stomach. Snails have thick, fleshy lips that get a sucker-like grip, while a kind of gristly tongue, bearing thousands of teeth, acts as a file, or rasp, on the vegetable substance. The common garden snail has nearly 15,000 teeth on its file, arranged in 135 rows, and, as the front rows wear away, new rows appear from behind to replace them.

SPEEDS STUPENDOUS

THE Earth we live on flies through space at wonderful speeds. (Do not overlook that s on the end of speed.) She is rushing round and round the Sun in a dizzy maypole dance at eighteen miles a second, which is 20 *times swifter than the swiftest shell can fly from the deadliest modern gun.* Yet this is but her first motion through space ; it is only a beginning. Most of you will know, or will have heard of *Vega*, the brightest star in the northern heavens, which is almost straight over our English heads on summer nights. Well, in company with the other planets of the solar system, the Sun is hauling the Earth and ourselves towards this beautiful bluish star at the rate of 700 miles a minute— ten times further in a minute than a crack express train gets in an hour. But in the

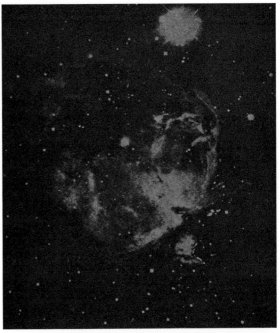

[*From a photograph taken at the Yerkes Observatory.*

THE GREAT NEBULA IN ORION.

The great spiral nebulæ, of which the nebula in Orion is one, are nearly all rushing away from us *at thousands of miles a second, millions of miles an hour.*

heavens, these to us terrifying speeds are just ordinary jog-trots. Still more amazing is the speed with which the Sun pursues its own gigantic orbit. It is drawing us round the hub of the galaxy at 200 miles a second, or about 2,300 times faster than a record-breaking motor car can travel. Is it not one of the wonders and mysteries of life that we should all be passengers every day of our lives on such a stupendous voyage at such spellbinding speeds without our being directly aware of it in any way ?

Even 200 miles a second is, nevertheless, far from being the highest known speed in the Universe. The great spiral nebulæ are the road hogs of the sky. They are nearly all rushing away from us at *thousands of miles a second, millions of miles an hour.*

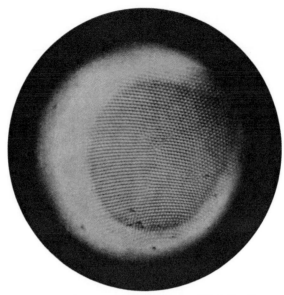

THE EYE OF A BEETLE.

Wonders of the Microscope

By ELLISON HAWKS.

AMONG the wonders revealed by the microscope there can be few that surpass in beauty the wing of a butterfly. Even to the unaided eye the colouring is very beautiful; in the microscope, though with a low power, it is enhanced a thousand times. The wings are seen to be composed of delicate membranes, stretched on a kind of fairy framework, called the " nervures."

If we take hold of a butterfly's wing we find our fingers covered with powder. This powder is composed of tiny scales, tens of thousands of which cover the membrane. The formation of the wing resembles the roof of a house, with its hundreds of slates supported by laths and joists. The scales are held to the wing by roots, and they lie upon the wing in rows, overlapping each other, just as do the slates of a roof. It is because of these scales that butterflies are said to belong to the order of *Lepidoptera*, a name derived from the Greek word *lepis*, meaning " a scale."

The accompanying Colour Plate shows a portion of about $\frac{1}{16}$ inch diameter of a tiny white dot in the " eye-spot " of the fore-wing of a Peacock Butterfly. The scales of a butterfly's wing obtain their

W.B.N.   C colouring from pigment, or colouring matter, actually embodied in them, just as a flower is coloured. This is not Nature's only way of obtaining coloured effects, however, for the wings of some insects that are beautifully iridescent, or rainbow-hued, owe their colouring solely to their extreme thinness. The walls of a soap-bubble are similarly exceedingly thin, and they, too, are iridescent. The scales of the small Diamond Beetle, shown at the foot of the Coloured Plate, belong to this class.

Yet another of Nature's methods of obtaining colour effects is by covering an object with a large number of extremely narrow lines, or furrows, which break up white light into all the colours of the rainbow. A good example of this type is afforded by the minute feathers in the breast of a Humming Bird, shown on the Plate.

The microscope reveals a host of wonders even in the most common objects. A snow-flake, a piece of coal, a lump of sugar—almost any object that we may choose, will show some details of interest when examined. Take, for instance, a thin slice of a potato, which we find to be composed of cells, each containing a number of oval objects. By applying a solution of iodine—that antiseptic yellow fluid that smarts so terribly when placed on a cut—the oval objects at once change to a beautiful blue colour. This proves that they are grains of starch, for no other substance will change to blue in this manner when iodine is applied. Starch grains are found in many other plants, especially in wheat, oats, arrowroot,

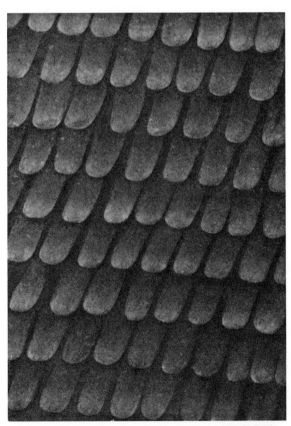

[Harold Bastin.

SCALES ON THE WING OF A BUTTERFLY, AS REVEALED BY THE MICROSCOPE.

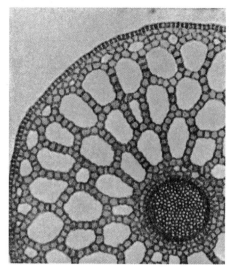

SECTION OF A PLANT STEM (MARE'S-TAIL),
showing a simple arrangement of cell structure.

Indian corn, sago, and tapioca.

In our walks we generally give stagnant ponds a wide berth, because they are sometimes covered with green slime that gives off an offensive odour on a hot summer's day. If we have a microscope, however, it is well worth while holding a handkerchief to the nose and braving these discomforts to obtain a jar of water from the pond. When we get this jar home and examine a few drops of the water under the microscope we find that our inconvenience is well repaid, for the water is full of the most amazing wonders.

Among the first things we are almost certain to see are bright-green objects of various sizes and shapes. These are called "Desmids," and they are well-known microscopic plants. The plants in our gardens and greenhouses form only a small proportion of the plant-life of the world, and the owner of a microscope is able to find minute plants similar to the Desmids in what seem to be the most unlikely places. A rotting fence or an old tree-trunk will probably yield more varieties of

microscopic plant-life than there are examples of the higher orders in the whole of the famous gardens at Kew.

The Desmids are a large family of plants composed of one cell only, and live in fresh water. Their bright-green colour enables them to be recognized at once as belonging to the plant-world. This distinction is useful to remember, since sometimes it is almost

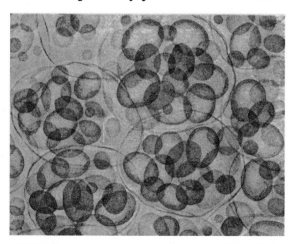

SECTION OF A POTATO,
showing cells containing starch grains.

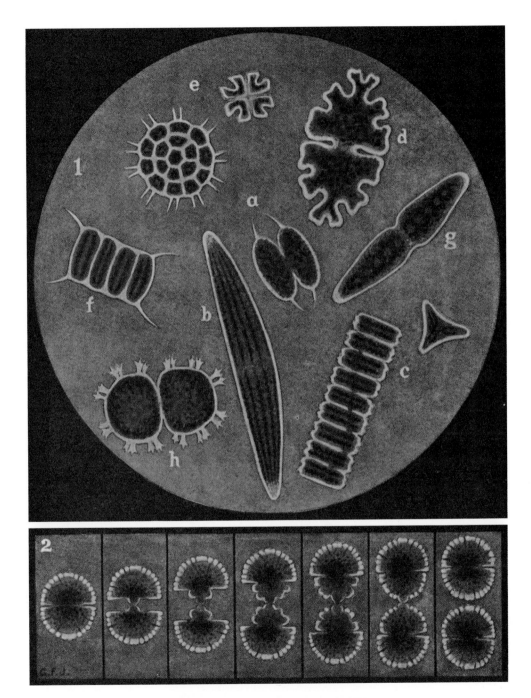

WONDERS OF THE MICROSCOPE.

VARIOUS SPECIES OF DESMIDS, TINY MICROSCOPIC PLANTS FOUND IN POND WATER.

The lower diagrams show the division of a single cell into two individual Desmids.

(From a painting by G. Fisher-Jones.)

impossible to decide, from its appearance alone, whether an object is vegetable or animal.

Desmids, which are of all shapes, have been divided into groups

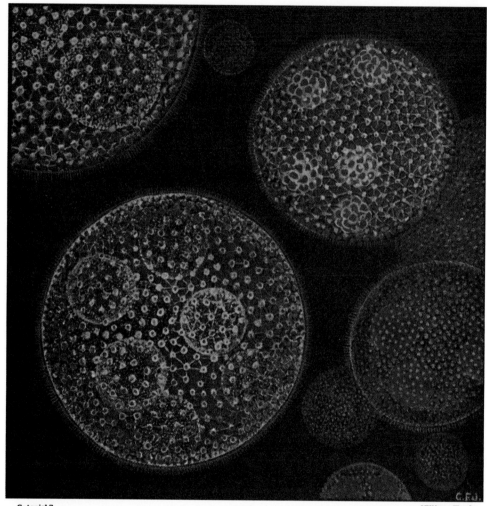

A BEAUTIFUL MICROSCOPIC PLANT THAT MOVES FROM PLACE TO PLACE.

Volvox globator is a microscopic plant found in ponds. The globe-shaped *Volvox* is composed of delicate lace-like tracery. Within may be seen the young ones, sometimes six or eight in number. This wonderful plant has the power to move from one place to another.

(From a painting by G. Fisher-Jones.)

to help in their classification. Some resemble a cucumber; others appear to be composed of several cells joined together; others, again, resemble part of a bamboo-cane with notched edges.

One of the most wonderful facts about these tiny plants is the way

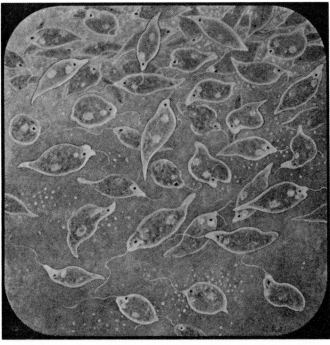

MICROSCOPIC POND LIFE.
Euglena viridis near the surface of a stagnant pond.
(*From a painting by G. Fisher-Jones.*)

they multiply. When fully grown, a Desmid will divide into two portions, each of which commences to grow, and becomes in time a fully grown Desmid, only in turn to divide again. In this manner Desmids illustrate the simplest method of reproduction in Nature, that of cell-division.

If we are lucky, we shall find in our drop of water examples of *Volvox globator*, a ball of lace-like tracery, infinitely more delicate than a spider's web. *Volvox* glides gracefully through the water by means of long *cilia*, or gossamer-like hairs, projecting from the green spots in its lace-like covering. This power of movement was the cause of *Volvox* at one time being classed in the animal kingdom. Now, however, it is recognized as being a true plant, but possessing the unusual power, for a plant, of being able to move from place to place.

Looking through the outer covering of *Volvox*, we are often able to see smaller green globes within. These are the young Volvoces, and sometimes even a third generation may be seen within the young Volvoces themselves. The young Volvoces eventually break through the sphere in which they were born and commence life on their own account.

In our jar we find a small portion of the leaf of some water-plant floating on the surface. Placing it under the microscope, we see it is covered with *Vorticellæ*, tiny cup-shaped bodies on long stalks, resembling a bunch of microscopic lilies-of-the-valley. *Vorticellæ* are not plants, however, but animals, so that we have the curious fact that in the microscopic world some plants (as *Volvox*) are able to move from place to place, whilst some animals grow on stalks! If the microscope be given a sharp tap, these stalks contract into spirals and draw the cup-shaped bodies to the base.

Vorticellæ obtain their food by setting up currents in the water, which passes through a small hole in the animalcule's body. The water is "strained" by a special appliance, and the food is thus extracted.

A somewhat similar class of object is *Stentor*, the trumpet-animalcule, which is generally of a brilliant green colour. It resembles the mouth of a cornet, and is a very beautiful object, as you can judge by the illustration on the next page.

Although we could fill several volumes in describing the wonders in a drop of water, we have space to mention only one other example. For this let us choose a curious-looking object, resembling a kind of little tube composed of numbers of rounded pellets placed in regular rows one above the other and not unlike a wall of tiny bricks. This is *Melicerta ringens*, the brick-building *Rotifer*.

As we watch, we see a tiny head appear above the

[*Ellison Hawks.*

MICROSCOPIC POND LIFE.

(1) *Melicerta ringens*, the brick-making *Rotifer* referred to in the article.
(2) *Rotifer vulgaris*, another microscopic animal.
(3) *Paramœcium aurelia*, a beautiful and delicate example of pond life.
(4) A young *Melicerta* that has been placed in coloured water and made to form bricks of various tints.
(*From a painting by G. Fisher-Jones.*)

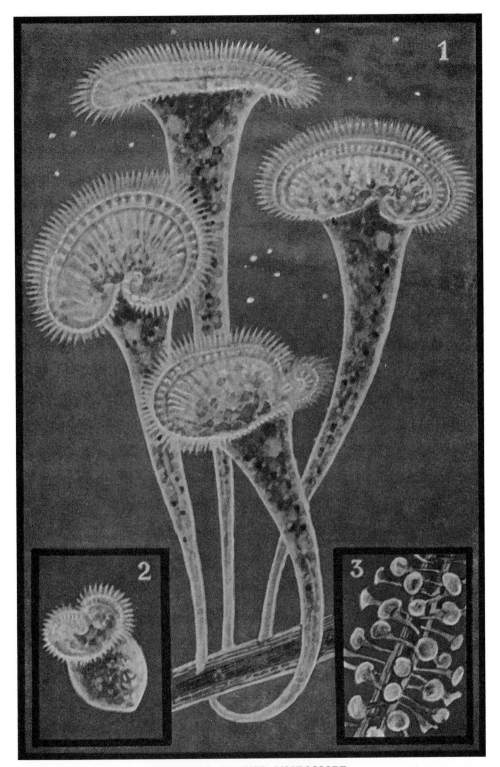

WONDERS OF THE MICROSCOPE.

Stentor Roeselii, the trumpet animalcule. This wonderful microscopic animal is rooted to a branch or leaf (as at 3). At certain times, however, it detaches itself (as at 2), and moves rapidly through the water by means of its *cilia*, or fine hair-like appendages.

(From a painting by G. Fisher-Jones.)

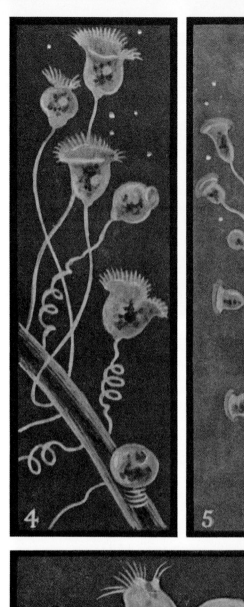

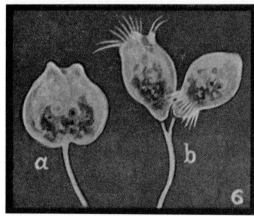

G.F.J.

WONDERS OF THE MICROSCOPE.

Other forms of microscopic animals include *Vorticella nebulifera* (4) and *Carchesium polypinum*, a tree-like animal (5) resembling a bunch of lilies-of-the-valley. Fig. 6 shows that *Vorticellæ* multiply by self-division. In *a* this division is commencing, and in *b* we see an individual about to detach itself. Fig. 7 is a *Vorticella* completely detached and freely swimming in search of a new home.

(From a painting by G. Fisher-Jones.)

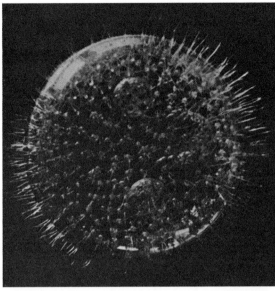

Most of the Protozoa are too small to be seen by the naked eye, but their beauty, as revealed by the microscope, is marvellous.

wall, apparently peeping over to see if the coast is clear. Its owner seems satisfied, and the head is fearlessly raised, expanding until it resembles a small silver pansy. Below the " petals " is a kind of chin, and beneath this again is the wonderful apparatus with which *Melicerta* makes the bricks for its " house." It gathers the necessary material from the surrounding water and passes it down narrow grooves to a minute cup, which acts both as a mixing chamber and a mould. Here the particles are welded together and the resulting " brick " placed on the rim of the tube. Brick after brick is placed in position until the " house " is built.

A very interesting experiment is to place a few drops of colouring matter—such as cochineal —in the water. This causes *Melicerta* to make red bricks. A drop of ultramarine in the water changes the colour of the bricks to blue, and so we are able to make *Melicerta* build a house of whatever combination of coloured bricks we wish !

Another example, with spines. The creatures abound in stagnant water, as ponds, and in the sea.

A Great Anteater, from South America, displays his two
feet of tongue. The tongue is used to draw its natural food,
ants, from deep holes and narrow crevices.

SO LIFE GOES ON

THE amœba is one of the lowest forms of animal life. It is
invisible to the naked eye, and is just a tiny speck of naked
protoplasm, or life matter. It feeds with any part of its substance,
and is found in stagnant water, or on wet mud.

In common with many other single-celled animals, the amœba
multiplies by dividing itself into halves, each half then growing to
its full size. The strange thing about this simple method of reproduction, is that these tiny animals never die a natural death. Barring
accidents, their substance continues to divide again and again to
form others just like themselves. As some of them can undergo
division every few hours, the earth would soon become full of them,
were it not that they are being continually devoured by other animals.

These single-celled animals are called *protozoa*—or early animals
—and some of them secrete tiny shells of pretty forms around their
substance. The *foraminifera* make calcareous, or chalky shells, while
the *radiolaria* form siliceous, or glass-like structures of amazing beauty.
These marine forms are, nevertheless, just simple amœbæ with a shell
covering.

All life is cell-life, and the many-celled forms, called *metazoa*—
or later animals—have their cells specialized to build the various
parts of their anatomy. The metazoa range from sponges and hydras
to worms, and eventually to mammals.

SO LIFE GOES ON

A slug and its eggs.   [Dorien Leigh.

With the advance of more complex anatomy, reproduction by division gradually gives place to cells specialized for that function—egg cells. The sea-anemone may, however, split into two, or bud out several young from various parts of the surface of its body. Also, it may spread wide its tentacles and eject a few tiny anemones from its mouth. Lastly, it may produce eggs.

The egg of an animal does not necessarily produce a miniature of its parents. As we have seen in the case of the frogs and newts, their eggs develop a tadpole. Similarly, the egg of a butterfly, or a moth, hatches out a caterpillar; although some insects' eggs, as those of earwigs and crickets, give birth to young of much the same form as their parents, but which are destitute of wings. Their wings develop gradually as growth proceeds. Where there are distinct changes, as caterpillar, chrysalis, and finally the winged fly, the metamorphosis is complete. In the lower insects, which reach their full development by a gradual growth, it is incomplete.

Turning to the warm-blooded animals. The birds show a direct course from the hatching of the egg to the young bird, which, with growth, soon becomes a replica of its parents. The mammals protect and develop their eggs in the maternal body, so that their offspring appear as living young.

There are, however, two Australian mammals, the Duck-billed Platypus, and the Porcupine Ant-eater, which really do lay eggs, but these animals represent the most primitive types of mammalian life. They may be regarded as living fossils.

By courtesy of]   [Australian Trades Publicity.
A Duck-billed Platypus — an Australian egg-laying mammal. Note the bill and the nostrils.

Ripe " fruit " capsule of the Rose-bay Willow herb.   *Left :* Ready
to dehisce (burst open).   *Right* : After being touched, scattering its
feathery, wind-borne seeds.

HOW PLANTS DISPERSE THEIR SEEDS

JUST as animals must produce young in order to carry on their
race, so must plants form seeds that they may multiply and
cover the earth.   These seeds are, however, often produced in great
numbers and we see that this is necessary when we realize how many
may be eaten by birds or fail to reach ground suitable for germination.
Large numbers of seeds alone will not ensure success.   Suppose that
all the seeds of an Elm were to drop down on to the ground immediately
under the branches of the parent tree.   If only fifty of these seeds
germinated and lived, in a year or two there would not be sufficient
light or moisture for all of them, and overcrowding is just as bad
for plants as for human beings.   The Elm seeds are specially formed
to avoid this congestion.   Each seed is fixed in the centre of an
oval, flat wing which enables it to be carried quite long distances
by the wind.   In this way the seeds are dispersed over a wide area
and those that fall on suitable ground are able to germinate and grow
to maturity.

Wind is quite an efficient means of dispersal, especially when
the seed is particularly adapted for this means of transport.   The
Sycamore is a good example of another wind-dispersed seed.   The
seeds are joined in pairs and each seed has a long, thin, wing-like
appendage.   When it becomes detached from the tree, this double

HOW PLANTS DISPERSE THEIR SEEDS

THE LESSER CELANDINE.
In addition to usual methods of reproduction,
small bulbils drop off occasionally and grow into
separate plants.

samara, as it is called, spins round as it travels through the air and is carried some distance from the parent. Other trees with similar winged seeds are the Ash and the Maple.

Among the smaller plants, the common Dandelion with its head of white-plumed seeds, is a well-known wind-dispersed plant. Attached to each seed by a stalk is a parachute-like mass of feathery hairs by means of which the seed can float about in the air for a considerable time. When a house is pulled down in the middle of London, miles away from open fields, it is surprising

how quickly Dandelions, Willow-herbs, Thistles and other weeds spring up on the empty site. The seeds of these plants must have been carried considerable distances by the wind.

The seeds of most aquatic plants are of necessity dispersed by water, those of the Water Lily have air-spaces which enable them to remain afloat until they have drifted some distance from the parent plant. The fruits of the Coco-nut Palm are often carried hundreds of miles by ocean currents to germinate on some distant shore. They are not

Photos]   [H. Bastin.
" AEROPLANES."
Air-borne fruits of the Maple, Sycamore, Ash
and Lime.

then smooth and round as we know them in shops and on the fair ground, but are covered with a thick, oval, fibrous coat which enables them to float.

THE GARDEN BALSAM (TOUCH-ME-NOT).
How the " explosive ". fruit scatters its seed.

The fruit of the B u r d o c k (*Arctium Lappa*) is provided with hooked bristles which enable it to hang on to the coats of sheep or other animals as they brush by. The " bur " will probably be carried many miles before it becomes detached or the animal rubs it off. The seeds of many other plants are provided with hooks or prickles by which they may become entangled in the fur of animals and even in the feathers of birds, thus becoming very widely dispersed. One frequently finds the little fruits of Goose-grass (*Galium Aparine*) sticking to ones clothes after a country walk. The fruits of the Herb Bennet (*Geum urbanum*) and the Hounds'-tongue (*Cynoglossum officinale*) also have the hooked and curved prickles which adapt them for animal dispersal.

Animals assist with seed dispersal in other ways. The soft outer pulp of the Mistletoe seed is eaten by thrushes, but it is also very sticky, so that the hard seeds become attached to the bird's beak. The thrush then rubs its beak on a branch and the seeds are thus transferred to the tree on which they will germinate and produce the Mistletoe. Attrac-

Photos]   [*H. Bastin.*

HOOKED FRUITS AND SEEDS.
Top : Stages of development of the fruit of the Geum. *Bottom* (*left to right*) : Cleavers, Woodruff and Burdock.

tively - coloured, fleshy-fruits such as the Yew-berry, Raspberry, Mulberry are very largely dispersed by birds. The fruits are eaten by the birds, but the seeds have a hard covering and are not digested. They pass unharmed through the digestive tract of the bird and are

THE " WATER HYACINTH."
Remarkable " floats " formed by swollen leaf-stems.

eventually deposited with the droppings.

The seeds of many plants do not depend on the help of birds or of the wind for their dispersal. They possess mechanical means of their own for this end. In Gorse and in many other members of the Bean Family (*Leguminosæ*) a tension is created as the seed pod becomes dry and ripe, until the slightest touch will cause the pod to burst open, throwing the seeds to a considerable distance. Everyone knows how the little ripe capsules of the Balsam or Touch-me-not (*Impatiens Noli-me-tangere*) explode when they are touched.

One of the most remarkable examples of a mechanically-dispersed fruit is that of the Squirting Cucumber (*Ecballium Elaterium*), which grows wild in Italy. As the small oval, green fruit becomes ripe, the seeds contained in a sticky pulp inside become very much compressed by the inner wall of the fruit. Finally, at the slightest touch, the fruit will spring from its stalk and with a whizzing noise the seeds will shoot out to a distance of several feet.

Photos]   *[H. Bastin.*
THE SQUIRTING CUCUMBER.
When touched it squirts forth to some distance fluid and seeds.

Trees that have become solid rock—Arizona, United States of America.

TREES TURNED TO STONE

ARIZONA, one of the United States of America, has many wonderful sights. In it is to be found the Grand Canyon, that most wonderful of gorges through which the Colorado flows. But it has other things to show, which carry the mind back into ages far removed from ours. It is indeed not four hundred years since the Spaniards first explored Arizona, and its history begins, but in the books of Nature much was written before then. One story still lives in one rare sight which meets the traveller ; he comes in his journeys upon a petrified forest which covers more than ten square miles. It will not be hard to know what a " petrified forest " is like if we think of it as a mass of trees turned to stone. We know how trees become coal and lie deep in the earth, or near to the surface. But these trees are lying there, in the open, like huge logs, where they have been for long ages ; long before the Spaniards saw them they were as they are to-day.

TREES TURNED TO STONE

Nobody can be sure how this came about ; but scholars who have studied this forest tell us how once there may have been a tornado of tremendous power, which swept out by their roots large numbers of trees, and hurled them into this wild place.

[Fox Photos.

Another view of the petrified forest, Arizona.

A tornado is not simply a very strong wind ; it is a wind which as it moves swiftly along turns still more swiftly round and round on its own axis. Americans in certain parts of their great country dread the coming of the tornado, which usually destroys all that is in its way except the very strongest of buildings. Such a tornado, mightier than others, quite possibly tore up these trees, and left them.

In the ages that followed, the fibres of wood were apparently filled with minerals and the great trees became in time like minerals themselves. It is for all the world as if some great magician had fixed them there, turned them to stone and left them for ages and ages till Man arrived, and endeavoured to read their story.

STRANGER THAN FICTION

OUR WONDERFUL HOME—THE EARTH

THE rocky face of the Earth is as ever-changing, alive and sensitive as your face or mine. Our native land is disappearing before our very eyes. Do you realise, for instance, that the Thames (mostly in the form of mud, sand and dissolved chalk) washes over 40,000 cubic feet of the hills and fields of Old England into the North Sea *every 24 hours?* Which in twelve months amounts to a huge lump nearly twice the size of the great super-ship " Queen Mary."

Similarly, the mighty Mississippi empties every year into the Gulf of Mexico, *more of the solid rock substance of North America than could be transported by the biggest railway system in the world.* This whole-sale wearing down and destruction of the countryside is being carried out by rain, storms and rivers the world over, and geologists call it denudation. Geology is the name of that branch of Science which treats of these things and the Earth (*gē* is Greek for " the earth ") in general and endless are the wonders it keeps bringing to light. It has been found recently that, at

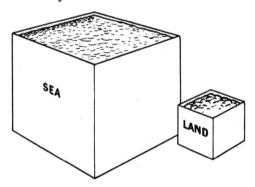

A tank measuring 690 miles each way would be needed to hold all the sea in the world, but all the dry land would go into a box 300 miles each way.

present rates of denudation, *there will be no dry land at all left in the world in ten million years' time at most.* It will all have vanished beneath the waves. And remember, here, that ten million years in the life of the Earth represents only about four months in the life of a man. Furthermore, there is plenty of room in the sea for all the land, since the water on our planet amounts to twelve times the bulk or volume of the land. In fact, all the continents, mountains, forests and cities of the Earth could be sunk in the Pacific Ocean without leaving a trace. Sometimes the process of destruction is rapid and violent almost beyond belief. In August, 1900, a sudden rainstorm cut a channel twenty feet deep in a Welsh mountainside in a few hours. In the famous Bishop Rock lighthouse, a bell weighing three hundredweight was once wrenched off one hundred feet above high water by mountainous sea waves during a violent storm. Among the Shetland Islands, enormous twelve-ton blocks of rock have been actually hacked and quarried out of the cliffs seventy feet above high tide, by the fury of winter breakers.

Every acre of Britain has more than once been at the bottom of the sea. And has, therefore, risen from the sea as often. At this very moment territories are doing this very same thing. Almost the whole of Japan is in slow motion either up or down. Parts are sinking down to sea-level while other parts are rising above sea-level at accurately measured rates. During the New Zealand earthquake of 1931, the harbour shallowed so swiftly that ships riding at anchor there had to race full steam ahead for the open sea to save themselves from going aground. The shallowing of the waters, of course, was caused by a quick rising of the harbour bed. Nature *can* hurry, you see, when she likes. Lake Michigan, one of the five Great Lakes of fresh water on the Canada-United States border, *is being slowly tilted like a mammoth, perfectly poised see-saw*—up at the north end, down at the south. And at present rates, less than six hundred years will suffice to drown the great city of Chicago.

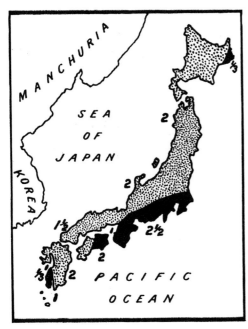

UPS AND DOWNS IN JAPAN.
Some parts of Japan are steadily sinking, while other parts are rising. The figures show the rate in inches per ten years. Black areas are sinking, and dotted areas are rising.

Recent earthquakes in California are attributed, in part at least, to great blocks of the Earth's crust slipping and pushing in opposite directions against each other. According to one eminent authority, for one hundred miles south of San Francisco *the countryside is bodily creeping south*, whilst still farther south, over a considerable area, *the hills are actually moving northward*. The Moon causes tides not only in the waters of the Earth, but also in the solid crust of the Earth (to a lesser extent, of course, rocks being more rigid than water)—the lands we live on. *St. Paul's Cathedral moves eighteen inches up and down every day without anybody being able to feel it.* Circular railway tunnels and tubes under London's streets and houses *go slightly oval or egg-shaped at high tide.* So sensitive and yielding is the Earth's surface, indeed, that a speech-day assembly of a couple of hundred people has been known actually to lower the grounds of an English college by one inch. The lawn rose to its normal level again after the gathering dispersed. About twenty minutes after the great Assam earthquake of June, 1897, the whole of Europe gently rose and fell on land waves, waves of solid rock, thirty-five miles long and twenty inches high. Though easily detectable and measurable

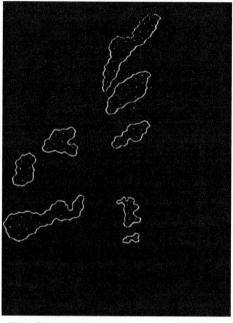

The British Isles as they were during the Cretaceous or Chalk period, somewhere about 80 million years ago.

by modern instruments, the cradle-like motions could not be felt by the unaided human senses because the waves were so enormously long in proportion to their height. A sea wave, indeed any wave, can hardly be either seen or felt if it is more than one hundred times longer than it is high.

Happily, therefore, Europeans saw nothing and felt nothing of the deadly undulations which passed on to encircle the whole globe before eventually dying away.

The amazing facts of science are far stranger than the fictions of our most imaginative romance.

The oceans are always receiving the ruins and debris of the land.

The British Isles as they are to-day.

216

But the ruins of the old are the raw materials of the new. Though old Father Neptune is fast destroying the continents, his is the vast unseen workshop where future continents are being made.

Nearly all the rocks of Britain, the rocks under our feet, our cities and our highways, were formed on the sea-floor. In crumbling and carrying them off to the sea, rivers are only returning them to the place of their birth.

" Change and decay in all around, I see," is not just the lament of a famous hymn ; it is the very voice of modern geology. As the poet Tennyson says :

> " The hills are shadows, and they flow
>   From form to form, and nothing stands ;
>   They melt like mists, the solid lands,
> Like clouds they shape themselves and go."

—In Memoriam.

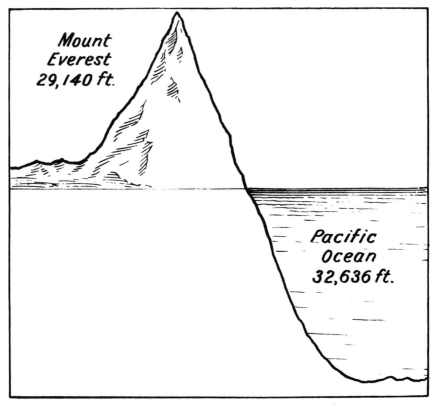

Diagram comparing the depths of the Pacific Ocean
with the highest mountain—Mount Everest.

PLANTS THAT "SLEEP"

THE so-called "sleep" movement of plants, the nocturnal drooping of the leaves and the closing of the flowers, have no connection with the sleep of animals. The plant must guard against excessive loss of heat during the cool hours of the night and to do this it reduces the exposed area of its leaves by folding them together. The Wood-sorrels (*Oxalis*) and the Clovers (*Trifolium*) show this "sleep" movement very well; their leaflets droop even in daytime if there is a drop in temperature, and at night the leaflets are folded so that the under surfaces are touching.

The closing of flowers at night is also a protective arrangement. In this case in districts where there is a heavy dew, if the flowers did not close up at night, the moisture would saturate the pollen, causing the grains to swell up and burst. Each plant has a definite time for opening its flowers and also a fixed time for going to "sleep." Some flowers rise very early in the morning. Wild roses open their flowers between 4 and 5 a.m. The Morning Glory (*Ipomœa purpurea*), a climber often seen in our gardens, opens its buds at about 4 a.m. At a more reasonable hour, between

[*By Ewing Galloway, N.Y.*

A night-blooming Cactus (*Cereus*). Its fragrant white flowers open about midnight.

eight and nine, we find the Gentians, Wood-sorrels and Speedwells coming to life. The Tulips do not awake until between nine and ten, while the Cinquefoil is really lazy and does not open its buds until between eleven and twelve. In normal circumstances in this climate no plant opens its flowers between twelve noon and about six in the evening. About this time the Evening Primrose opens; later, between seven and eight, the Night-flowering Stock commences to scent the evening air. These night-flowering plants remain open all night, for they are pollinated by the night-flying insects, the moths; they close again early in the morning. The times of opening and closing of the flowers vary, of course, with different climates.

HUNTERS OF THE LATER ICE AGE.
(From a painting by F. Cormon.)

ICE OVER ENGLAND

ONE day, in a quiet and beautiful place in Sussex, I stopped to ask a child what the name of the village was. She answered, "Piltdown," and I thought at once of the ancient skull which was found there and takes its name from that place. Somewhere near that place Piltdown Man in ages far removed from ours lived ; and what a different world it must have been ! And what a different being he was ! And he, too, lived long ages before these hunters whom the artist has pictured to us.

Imagine that once England was a little like Greenland. The ice reigned in our pleasant and green land. There were glaciers just as there are in Switzerland to-day ; vast sheets of ice might fall into the valleys. It was a cold and dreary land. But there came a time when the reign of the Ice in our land came to an end. We must not think that one day all the creatures of the earth suddenly discovered that the change had come, as a summer comes after the winter. It was a slow, very slow retreat, but it was an important moment in the history of the being called Man, when the retreat was ending. Waves of new life came to these islands from the east of Europe. And it was in that later age, when the Ice was being defeated, that the shores of England looked like the shores of Greenland. It was, perhaps, to some part of that later ice age that these hunters belonged.

They had built no settled homes ; they lived in caves, and were clothed in skins. They hunted the reindeer, and the musk-ox, and other wild beasts, which, as the ice age drew to its close, removed themselves northward.

Why did these hunters come to these islands ? Why did they travel at all ? It is safe to suppose that some change had taken place in the climate of eastern Europe. Just as the creatures, mammoths and bears and reindeer, which were at home in the ice, when the warmer conditions came about, turned northward, so this creature Man also went where he could live most easily and where he could hunt his prey. Man as he was then was very different from Man as we know him ; but he had already learned the secret which gave him his victory over the other mighty creatures.

WONDERFUL FLIGHTS BY BUTTERFLIES AND MOTHS

NEARLY all of you must have heard of the wonderful flights or migrations of birds, but probably very few of you know that butterflies and moths can also fly long distances. Some butterflies and moths live only for a few days or a week or two at the most. Others live for several weeks or even months, and naturally it is only some of those with a fairly long life which can migrate. They may travel hundreds of miles, and having started in a particular direction they do not alter their course, even if the wind should happen to be against them. They fly over land and sea and occasionally alight

The Painted Lady.

on the decks of steamers, much to the surprise of passengers. Migratory swarms arrive in Britain from Africa and Europe in spring or early summer, but these are not such an amazing sight as the really enormous swarms seen in tropical countries. There, millions of butterflies may be seen all travelling in the same direction for hours, days or even weeks on end.

Scientists are not certain in many cases where the actual homes and starting places for these migratory flights of butterflies are situated ; nor can they tell how the insects manage to keep flying in the same direction once they start. These are some of the problems which perhaps one day some of you who become scientists may help to solve. The reason for the flight in many cases appears to be due to overcrowding and, therefore, a shortage of food in their breeding places. Many of the common white Cabbage Butterflies which appear in summer have flown over the Channel from France and Spain, and the Painted Lady Butterflies which spend the winter in Africa, fly to southern England in spring, some going on further north to Scotland, and a few reaching even Iceland.

[*Photos reproduced from " British Butterflies," F. W. Frohawk.*

A Cabbage White Butterfly depositing eggs on a leaf.

A male Three-spined Stickleback (*Gasterosteus aculeatus*) building a nest. He constructs it of water weeds and grasses and then persuades three or four female Sticklebacks to lay their eggs in it.

EGGS BY THE MILLION

FISH, shellfish, and insects lay the most eggs of all creatures. Many birds lay only one or two eggs a year, but nearly all fish produce thousands of them, and some even lay such millions of eggs that it is a wonder the surface of the sea has not become solid with fish a long time ago !

A big Cod lays 6,650,000 eggs each spring, but the parent fish make no nest to protect them, and just leave them floating in masses near the surface of the sea, while they swim away themselves to feed. Cod's eggs are nearly transparent, and about the size of small pin heads, so they do not show up very much in the sea. All the same, thousands of them are gobbled up by other kinds of fish, and thousands more are often destroyed by high winds and rough seas, and altogether very few ever hatch. Probably only about five or six Cod ever grow big out of all the millions of eggs laid by one mother each spring !

Some other fish lay even more eggs than the Cod. An Eel lays about 10,000,000, and another fish called a Ling, which is rather like a Cod, only it grows much longer, lays over 28,000,000 eggs a year.

Herrings do not need to lay nearly so many eggs, only about 30,000, because their eggs are heavy and sink down and stick to the shingly bed of the sea, so that other fish cannot easily find and eat them. Quite often, though, a shoal of Haddock will follow the Herrings while they are "spawning" and try to eat up their eggs before they sink into a safe hiding place.

Thousands of young Elvers (Eels) are greedily gobbled up by other creatures of the sea. When hatched, young elvers are transparent, flat and leaf-shaped.

A few fish, the little green Sticklebacks that live in rivers and estuaries, for instance, do make nests and take good care of their eggs, so they do not need to lay so many. The father Stickleback builds a little nest about the size of a golf ball, of water weeds and grasses, stuck together with some of his slime, and he persuades three or four female Sticklebacks to lay their eggs in it. Then he swims round and guards it most fiercely, fighting with the spines on his back and especially driving off the mothers, who try to get back and eat one another's eggs! Sea Horses also lay few eggs, perhaps only about a hundred a year, and the father Sea Horse carries these about for safety in a little pocket which grows on the front of his body. When the eggs hatch, the baby Sea Horses come floating out, four or five at a time, and they soon hide themselves among seaweed to avoid being eaten by other fish.

Oysters also lay great numbers of eggs, English ones about

1,000,000, but some kinds lay about 60,000,000 eggs, only these are so small that there is room for them all to be kept and protected inside the mother Oyster's shell. Here they hatch in about two days and start swimming about like minute white specks. Then, in another two or three days, tiny Oyster shells begin to grow on them and they turn first grey, then purple as they increase in size. Very soon these baby Oysters, or "spat" as they are called, must get away from the mother's shell and find homes for themselves, so little hairs

The young Oysters or "spat" no sooner make their appearance than many are devoured by other fish. When ten days old, they swim away from the mother by lashing the water with little hairs called "cilia." Later they stick down on stones or rocks and form Oyster beds.

called "cilia" grow out of their shells, and by lashing the water with these cilia they swim away. This happens when they are ten days old. Many of them are gobbled up by other creatures of the sea, but those that are left stick down on stones or rocks, or on pieces of wood put ready for them, and in this way new Oyster beds are formed.

DENIZENS OF THE DEEP.

In some deep-sea fish the light organs are arranged in definite patterns, glistening like jewels, or resembling the illuminated port-holes of a liner at night, thus helping, in all probability, other fish of the same kind to recognise each other and keep together in a shoal.

THE MAGIC OF THE HEAVENS.

An artist's impressions of the Sun, showing its corona ; Coggia's Comet ; the Planet Mars ; Saturn, with its rings ; and a " close-up " of the surface of the Moon.

PREHISTORIC ANIMALS.

    1.   *The Pterodactyl.* The latest of these creatures of which we have any knowledge had wings with a total expanse of eighteen feet.

    2.   *The Tyrannosaurus.* This dinosaur had a body forty feet in length, and his tail helped him to balance as he walked along swiftly on his hind legs.

CUTTLEFISH.

Cuttlefish are distinguished from the squids and octopods by their flat bodies and long, narrow fins. They live in shallow coastal waters of warm and temperate seas.

HOW A BIRD FLIES

Golden Eagle	Prehistoric Pteranodon (18 ft. wing-span)	Prehistoric Archaeopteryx
Flamingo	Albatross (10 ft. or more wing-span)	Pelican (Flying with head held back)
Pheasant	Diagram showing positions of a gull in flight	Roseate Spoonbill

KANGAROOS.

When the kangaroo is walking or standing upright, it uses its long, muscular tail as a fifth leg, or prop.
A big kangaroo, when hard pressed, can bound 25 feet or more and clear obstacles five or six feet high.